Horse Structure and Movement

HORSE STRUCTURE AND MOVEMENT

by

R. H. SMYTHE   MRCVS

Third Edition

Revised by

PETER GRAY   MVB, MRCVS

J. A. ALLEN
London

British Library Cataloguing in Publication Data

Smythe, Reginald H.
    Horse Structure and Movement. — 3Rev.ed.
    I. Title II. Gray, Peter
    636.1

ISBN 0-85131-547-X

© J. A. Allen & Co. Ltd, 1993

First published in 1967
by J. A. Allen & Co. Ltd.

Second edition published in 1972
Revised by Peter C. Goody, BSc, PhD, FLS.

First paperback edition published in 1975

Published in Great Britain in 1993 by
J. A. Allen & Company Ltd.,
1, Lower Grosvenor Place, Buckingham Palace Road,
London, SW1W 0EL

Typeset in Hong Kong by Setrite Typesetters Ltd.
Printed in Hong Kong by Dah Hua Printing Co. Ltd.

Contents

Acknowledgements

I would like to thank my publishers for their valued help and for giving me the opportunity to add my contribution to such a distinguished work. I would also like to thank Maggie Raynor for her excellent artwork.

To David Watson BA, MRCVS, I wish to extend my appreciation for his help with the sections dealing with the spine. It is to be hoped that, someday, he will transfer the great volume of his knowledge to writing, and enhance the benefit of books like *Horse Structure and Movement*. The horse world, and the veterinary profession, would be the richer for it.

Foreword

The first edition of this book was published in 1967 and was presented by R. H. Smythe MRCVS, '...for the layman rather than for the veterinary surgeon who has studied anatomy in far greater detail than is needed in this volume...' At that stage the book was composed of four main sections rather than chapters: The Bones of the Horse; The Surface of the Horse; The Horse at Rest and in Motion; Some Thoughts about Conformation. To these was added an appendix which comprised a series of articles previously published in *Horse and Hound*.

Dr. P. C. Goody BSc, PhD, FLS, revised the work extensively in 1975, adding a wider base of valuable anatomical detail and bringing the book to a standard that would have to appeal to anyone studying the horse as an athletic animal.

This second revision is aimed at collating the existing material into a more accessible form and, hopefully, expand the scope of what was already an excellent book. The format has now been changed into chapters rather than sections. This was necessary to broaden the discussion and eliminate the inevitable repetition that was caused by the appendices.

The first three sections of the earlier editions are largely unchanged in content, just form. More diagrams have been introduced to make the presentation more visual. The section on movement has been changed marginally to fall in line with modern research on the subject. The small extent of this is a tribute to the quality of Smythe's original manuscript and the excellent updating of Goody's work.

I have attempted to bring a wider clinical view to the basic anatomy and physiology involved. A greater accent has been placed on the back and the muscular system, and their influence on lameness. The part concussion plays in athletic injuries is also brought into context. I have also tried to broaden the section on conformation and to align this to the subject of soundness.

Recent decades have seen a wide development of disciplines such as physiotherapy and chiropractic manipulation. It is to be hoped that relevant authorities will bring some order into the manner in which these are applied and that there will be adequate standards of education required for those who treat horses. The present situation is far from ideal.

Peter Gray
Leinthall Earls, 1992

Technical Note

Throughout the book many of the technical, anatomical and Latin names and descriptions have been italicised the first time they appear to help the reader assimilate the text. Subsequently they are only italicised again for particular emphasis.

1 General Aspects of Structural Anatomy

Before we can understand how a horse performs and accomplishes all demanded of it, it is necessary to become familiar with structural anatomy and put this in context with the mechanics of movement — *kinematics*, or, more properly, *biomechanics* — so that we may see and anticipate the weaknesses commonly met.

In the past 30 odd years there has been a substantial change in the usage of horses. The working horse has largely gone but his place has been filled by an expansion of racing and leisure riding that promises to develop even further, besides which, a level of interest has been maintained in the heavier breeds that has assured their continuance too. For those who live in traditional horse-breeding countries there is the promise of new markets, and, even within our own shores, a growing interest from all sectors of the population. All this leads to a healthy future. However, there is a need to achieve new standards of care and understanding if our relationship with the horse is to prosper and thrive.

The study of movement as a science has found new importance in recent decades, partly because of difficulties in equine lameness diagnosis and the need for formalised methods of teaching on the subject. This has led to many innovative forms of technical gait analysis appearing, such as force and pressure plates, photography, etc. The purpose of these is to produce standards against which lame horses can be assessed, in a similar way to developments in human medicine. The hoped-for end result is that objective forms of assessment can be established for both teaching and diagnostic purposes. While these efforts are in their infancy and remain far from fulfilling objectives, the subject of locomotion is receiving a great deal of attention which may ultimately benefit the horse. Whatever else, this is likely to influence our understanding of the subject, and is adding to the vocabulary of the text we study here.

From a mechanical viewpoint, anatomy of the horse may be divided into the following sections:

    a. Head and neck
    b. Trunk, consisting of abdomen and thorax
    c. Four limbs
    d. A tail.

There is a common misconception that the horse is a natural jumper, possessed of a flexible and supple body capable of maintaining balance at all gaits and speeds. The reality is very different. In fact, of all athletic animals, the horse has been provided with a very inflexible carcass of great bulk and weight, which is solely propelled by the limbs, over ground and through air, as so much ballast. Apart from the trunk providing anchorage for muscles responsible for limb movement, its weight is a serious handicap to rapid and flexible progression, like a motor car with a very heavy chassis.

The head and neck may be regarded in two ways: first as a freely moving mass attached to an almost rigid body, designed to enable its owner to focus on and see a great deal it would miss were these less mobile. Secondly, the head acts as a heavy bob-weight suspended at

Fig. 1 The gallop in the greyhound and horse showing the different degrees of spinal flexion.

the end of a long, adjustable lever, the neck. This arrangement permits the animal to alter its centre of gravity, or balance, at will, thereby playing an essential part in overcoming the difficulty of hurling so much weight through space or propelling it effectively over ground at speed. Furthermore, while the head and neck play no direct part in progression, they give attachment to muscles originating in the forelimb and trunk that are critically involved in forelimb movement.

The thorax, which contains the heart and lungs, and the abdomen, containing the voluminous intestines and their contents, are together extremely weighty. Their shape and bulk are not conducive to speedy passage, and the degree of streamlining compatible with lung and heart room – variable with conformation – may have a marked influence on ability to race. For all practical purposes then, the horse's trunk may be regarded as a fixed weight propelled through space by the combined efforts of fore and hind limbs working in harmony.

The horse as we know it has passed through a long period of evolution, from the marsh-dwelling animal possessed of four, or even five

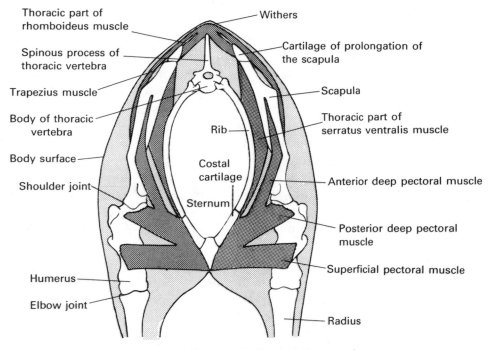

Fig. 2 Cross section of chest at the level of the scapula.

toes per foot to the single-digited soliped of today. Now, however, on firmer surfaces, it balances on four feet of small diameter, whose foothold is made even less secure by the addition of iron shoes. These feet have to support and balance the animal on the flat, up and down hill, when landing after a jump, and as a brake to slow the pace. On corners they hold balance, often at great speed, and must even contend with the interference that may occur, normally, in competition.

A close examination of finer anatomy might suggest the species is quite unsuited to all these tasks. However, whatever the limitations, the horse of today manages to carry out most of them remarkably well.

Before embarking on more detailed study we should consider aspects of general structure which are of distinct relevance to movement.

The Rigidity of the Spine

As already noted, the head and neck are highly flexible; so too is the tail a mobile part of the spinal system. However, between these extremities, the spine is a highly inflexible structure, capable of only minor movement *dorsoventrally* (up and down) and *laterally* (from side to side) (Fig. 3). This lateral flexion has been estimated to be limited to 15−20 cm (6−8 in) in the full length of the thoracic/lumbar/sacral region in a supple horse, with virtually none of this coming from the latter section. Qualified opinion has suggested that the figure is less than this, but 15−20 cm (6−8 in) is perfectly acceptable in the living animal (movement in this region in a dead animal is not comparable) and is clearly demonstrated during manipulation by experienced practitioners. But even this suggests that a horse depending on spinal flexion alone to complete a 90 degree turn would take several furlongs in which to achieve it. We know, however, that a horse pivots on its hind feet and *abucts* its limbs to achieve acute turns in confined areas.

Consider, too, a horse scratching its flank or quarter with its teeth. All the bending, virtually, is in the neck. There is very little help from the body which remains almost straight from withers to rump, the main assistance coming from abduction of the hind limb, moving it away as far as possible from the midline − but there is no curling of the spine.

Compare this movement with that of a dog or cat (Fig. 1); the difference is quite marked, and this has a significant influence on action. The horse is not a natural jumper with the spring and agility of carnivores, and it cannot roll itself into a ball as a cat or dog will do. In fact the total extent of dorsal and ventral movement of the spine — from withers to rump — is just as limited as lateral flexion; this is because nature simply did not design the area for its flexibility, but for its strength. However, this is not to say that slight dorsoventral flexion/ extension is not a part of normal movement at faster gaits and when jumping, but the common conception of the extent of this is exaggerated.

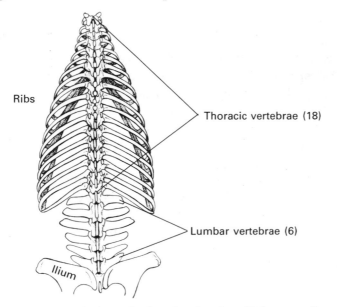

Ribs

Thoracic vertebrae (18)

Lumbar vertebrae (6)

Ilium

Fig. 3 Dorsal view of spine showing how little scope there is for lateral and dorsoventral movement.

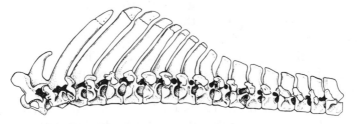

Fig. 3a Lateral view of thoracic vertebrae.

As a direct consequence of this anatomical reality, the incidence of spinal-origin lameness is an extremely significant factor in ridden horses today, and one we become more familiar with as time passes. The reason is that the rigid nature of the column means it is being asked to cope with explosive movements, in racing and jumping, that question its very integrity. While, fortunately, not many injuries sustained are of a permanent nature, a great number cause impaired movement and lameness, and the degree of deviation capable of causing this is known to be very slight. In many of these cases manipulation and physiotherapy are the best answer.

Spinal lameness is caused by interference to the anatomical integrity of the bony and soft tissue spinal structures. This may vary from fracture or luxation to minor deviations whose effect is muscle spasm, impaired movement, or inability to carry weight, these possibly reflecting pressure on spinal nerves. From a diagnostic point of view, the source is manually detectable on the surface of the spine, and there is generally an alteration of gait in one or more limbs associated with it. This problem is not experienced in any other animal to the same extent and should be a warning to us of the nature of the equine spine and what we are entitled to ask of it.

The strength of the spine is derived from a combination of bone, cartilage, ligament and muscle. Its weakness is exposed when horses without adequate muscular development or fitness are asked to perform exercises for which they are not adequately prepared. However, the same might be said of common muscular injuries − of which more later.

The Thoracic Sling

As will be noted from Fig. 2, the forelimbs are attached to the carcass in a way that suspends the thorax between them, as if in a sling. Alternatively, it could be said that the forelimbs are attached to the chest by muscle, ligaments and *fascia* only. This is because there is no *clavicle* in the horse, and no bony attachment between limb and thorax. The influence this has on locomotion is significant, allowing a type of movement which warrants comment. Firstly, as the thorax is suspended within this muscular sling, the body can actually be raised or lowered within it to an extent that can alter the centre of gravity up or down. Also it allows for *abduction* or *adduction* of the limbs in a way that has a significant influence on overall movement — a factor that plays an active part in dressage as well as in more everyday activities.

A horse bending as it gallops between obstacles will not curve its body through its length when it turns. Instead it adducts the forelimb nearest the object and rolls towards it, abducting the outer limb in relation to the thorax as it leans over. Therefore, if the horse pulls the left limb nearer the thorax, the body can actually roll to the left within the thoracic sling. The procedure is reversed when it turns the opposite way.

To a lesser degree this is what happens when a racehorse gallops at speed around Tattenham Corner. Its body does not actually bend, but rolls in its cradle while negotiating the turn, with the innermost limb tucked close to its ribs and the outer taking a slightly wider sweep than it would otherwise do. From this it might appear that the inner limb must slow down and the outer increase its speed. What really happens is that both move at about the same rate, but the outer takes a slightly longer stride.

Owing to this cradling of the thorax a horse is able to move both forward and sideways at the same time, and it is this freedom of abduction and adduction that plays so important a part in certain dressage movements. This ability to move the body in two directions at once has been attributed to an ability to bend the spine, but this is incorrect; most movement is created by the limbs.

Forelimb Extension

While the forelimbs are employed mainly to receive weight when the horse lands on the ground, they also have an important part to play in take-off and propulsion, as will be seen in later chapters. However, their ability to extend is limited by the muscular attachments of the shoulder and forearm to the body, and by the nature of the elbow and shoulder joints. Ultimately, this prevents extension of the limb, even at full gallop, from reaching beyond a point dropped vertically from the front of the muzzle.

Hind Limb Union with the Body

The hind limb, unlike the fore, is articulated to the skeleton by bony union at the hip joint — formed between femur and pelvis. Concussion is therefore transmitted through the pelvis directly to the spinal column, and is partly absorbed by the *intervertebral discs*, especially in the lumbar region. As already noted, this union is very different from the muscular union of forelimb and thorax.

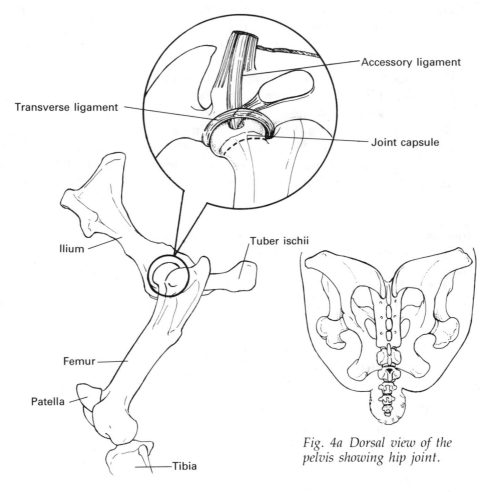

Accessory ligament

Transverse ligament

Joint capsule

Ilium

Tuber ischii

Femur

Patella

Tibia

Fig. 4a Dorsal view of the pelvis showing hip joint.

Fig. 4 Long union of the femur, pelvis and spine with detail of the hip joint.

Hind Limb Extension

The hind limbs are the power house of locomotion — though not the sole source — however, in contrast to carnivorous animals, where spinal flexibility allows for greater hind limb extension (Fig. 1), the horse is limited in this respect. In the greyhound, the *lumbar vertebrae* and *thoracic vertebrae* have considerable movement and this enables the whole length of the hind limb to be used in extension. Compare this to the spine of the horse, and, also, a femur that is closely coupled to the body by, and anatomically restricted by, heavy muscular and ligamentous attachments. Both facts limit extension, so that the furthest a hind limb can reach forward is seldom beyond a line dropped perpendicularly from the *umbilicus*. Also, while the animal can lash out behind, it is usually unable to cow-kick; forward movement being impeded by the presence of a ligament (the accessory ligament) joining the lower front of the pelvis with the hip joint itself.

Thus the horse gallops by generating most of its hind limb advancement through the stifle and hock joints. Of course, it also uses its spine to the full extent of its ability, limited as that may be.

The Vital Hock

One of the most important joints in the locomotory system, the hock, is also the hardest worked, for it plays an important part in the absorbtion of concussion.

Stifle and hock work in co-ordination, not individually. This double function is operated by means of two opposing sets of muscles, known as the *reciprocal mechanism*. The first set straightens (extends) the hock, the second flexes it (Fig. 5). This arrangement is on a par with that existing in the forelimb, and will be discussed later in relation to the *stay mechanism* which allows the horse to rest while standing.

When the hock is flexed, the stifle flexes simultaneously; when one extends so does the other. A horse straight in hock is also straight in stifle, and one with a very bent stifle will carry its hocks behind a line dropped perpendicularly from the seat bone.

A great deal of concussion in the hind limb is counteracted by means of combined hock and stifle flexion. The hock combines two kinds of joint: one capable of free unidirectional movement — a *ginglymus*, or hinge, joint; the other is only involved in more direct shock absorbtion.

Bog spavin (fluid in the joint) is a frequent consequence of faulty hock conformation. While it is possible that lameness may be slight or absent, the swelling indicates weakness and cannot be ignored.

Most common damage to the hock occurs in the two lower rows of flattened bones that lie on top of the cannon and medial small splint bone. This damage is expressed as degeneration and is the basis of true bone spavin seen on the inner side of the back of the hock at the level of its junction with the cannon.

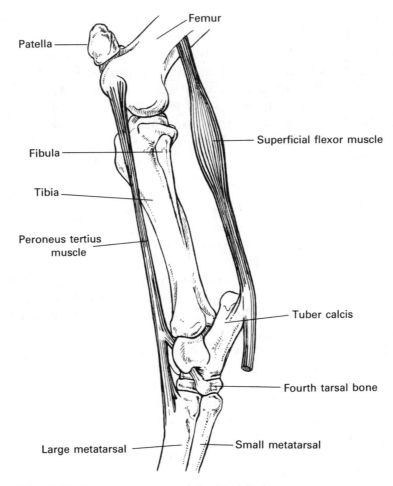

Fig. 5 Reciprocal apparatus of the hind limb.

The Stifle

This joint exists as a compound joint incorporating the unions between the femur and tibia and between the femur and patella. Its surfaces communicate through the *synovial sheaths* and work together in co-operation.

As aforementioned, this joint operates in reciprocal union with the hock, thus its significance in concussion absorbtion is important, especially as it distributes its effect to the large muscle masses attached to it and, through the femur, to the pelvis, body and spine.

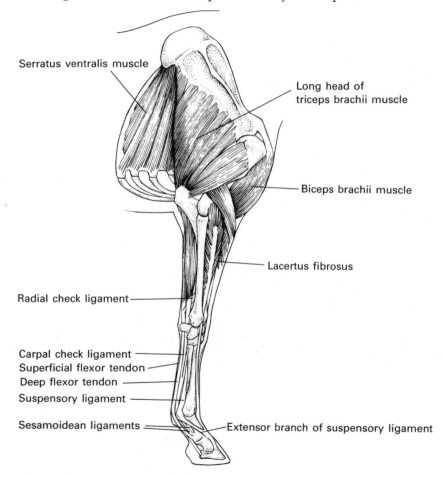

Serratus ventralis muscle

Long head of triceps brachii muscle

Biceps brachii muscle

Lacertus fibrosus

Radial check ligament

Carpal check ligament
Superficial flexor tendon
Deep flexor tendon
Suspensory ligament

Sesamoidean ligaments

Extensor branch of suspensory ligament

Fig. 6 Stay apparatus of the forelimb.

The horse's stifle is equivalent to the human knee and suffers from similar disabilities in the way of cartilage damage, luxations and inflammatory changes. In some cases the cause is strain or overwork of the joint, but in others it is due to hereditary unsoundness resulting from abnormal shaping of the joint.

The following factors will affect soundness of the stifle and hock:

a. The natural angulation of both joints
b. The condition of the synovial membranes
c. Maturity and nutrition
d. The age at which the animal first performs strenuous work.

Horses with straight hocks and stifles are better sprinters than those with greater angulation, because precocious speed results more from quick short strides rather than slow long ones. But straighter stifles are more likely to suffer from luxation of the patella — locking of the stifle — especially in immature horses. This kind of conformation is hereditary.

The Centre of Gravity

As already stated, the head and neck are substantial and free-moving at the front end of the trunk, therefore having a direct influence on the position of the centre of gravity. The thorax and forelimbs constitute a substantial part of the bony and muscular skeleton, although the organs contained within the thorax — the heart and lungs — are relatively light. The abdomen, including a weighty content of food material, is rigidly fixed to the thorax in front and only separated from it by the muscular diaphragm. Behind this are the hind legs and pelvis. Any need, therefore, to alter the centre of gravity for various exercises and positions is dependent on the mobility of the limbs and the counter-balancing effect of the head and neck.

We shall see later how to locate the centre of gravity, but it is evident from looking at the animal that this is closer to the front than the back of the trunk.

Concussion — Axial Compression Forces

The front limbs bear the main brunt of concussion because it is they that take the weight of the horse coming down from a jump, and also because they carry the greater proportion of body weight. This is reflected in the higher incidence of concussive lameness in the forelimbs, e.g. pedal ostitis, navicular disease, ringbones, sesamoiditis, splints, sore shins, carpitis, etc. Its influence is also affected to an extent by the fact that there is no natural angulation of the knee — as there is with the hock — to absorb concussion. However, if there were, the front leg would not be so stable when required to take the animal's weight as needed. This subject will be discussed in greater detail later.

Primary Muscular Lameness

Muscular lameness, resulting from primary rupture of muscle fibres, is of great importance, but, because it only tends to cause lameness for a limited period, its significance is often ignored. Within a matter of days of initial injury, the animal returns to a relative degree of soundness, and the accompanying alteration of gait is either not seen or disregarded. Yet the importance of this alteration is significant because it commonly leads to secondary lameness, which may often be expressed by way of tendon ruptures or injury to more rigid structures of the limbs. The common sites of muscular injury will be discussed in depth later.

Incidence of Lameness

Lameness is more common in the fore than hind limbs. This is attributed to the weight-bearing function of the forelegs, particularly as these are subjected to a force estimated at many times the horse's bodyweight when landing over a jump. Thus the bony and ligamentous structures of the foot, pastern, fetlock, cannon and knee are all exposed to direct concussive effects.

Hind limb lameness is more attributable to the spring-coil functions of the stifle and hock, and to the great muscle masses of the quarters and pelvis that help to raise the weight of the animal from the ground when asked.

In practice, muscular injuries and disturbances of spinal column anatomy are the most common sources of lameness encountered today. This is not far removed from the situation of the human athlete; the difference being that the human athlete is unable to perform with muscular or back pain, but the horse is often expected to through ignorance of his suffering.

The Skeleton

A detailed study of the skeleton will reveal the bones, their position and relationships, and enable examination of each one individually with regard to the *tuberosities* and *projections* which are detectable on the contours of the surface.

Bones carry projections and hollows for a variety of purposes:

a. Terminal enlargements are mostly involved in the formation of joints.
b. Surface projections give attachment to muscles.
c. Hollows and depressions may facilitate the movement of overlying structures, or, as in the case of the *olecranon fossa* at the back of the lower end of the *humerus*, accommodate another bony structure; in this example the *olecranon process* of the *ulna*.
d. Others, the skull and pelvic bones for example, have as their purpose the protection of essential parts such as the brain or reproductive organs.

A great many bones, or parts of them, may be palpated in their positions beneath the skin, and the ensuing descriptions and diagrams should help to associate surface characteristics with underlying bony structures.

Finally, to illustrate what has been said in this chapter, consider that a 14 hh pony may be able to execute a figure-of-eight during a hand-canter, without checking, in less than four body lengths, making use of the thoracic sling, hock flexion and its ability to pivot on the hind feet; the body remaining relatively rigid during the whole movement. The head and neck not only decide the direction in which the body shall travel, but also help to maintain equilibrium by calculated disposal of their joined weight. Through the course of the book we shall try to explain how this happens in greater detail.

2 The Bones of the Head

The Design of the Head and Neck

From a purely architectural standpoint the horse's head is elongated and bulky; much of this bulk being associated with the teeth and jaws and areas of bone associated with jaw muscle attachment. Thus, it would appear, the large size is related to feeding mechanisms; and it is probable the length of the neck was designed to meet the same basic priority. The horse is a grazing animal by nature, for which purpose the neck must be long enough so that the ground can be reached without difficulty.

This same design also allows the head and neck to act as an oscillating pendulum at the front, permitting changes in the distribution of body weight and maintenance of balance both when standing and moving, or even when the body is suspended in the air over a jump. By raising or lowering the head it is possible to alter the centre of gravity, while, by moving it a little to one side or the other, equilibrium can be maintained, even when rounding corners at speed.

The Skull

Of the numerous bones which make up the skull, those on the outside are mostly flattened and are united along their edges during early life by cartilage which later becomes replaced by bone. If the skull of a foal is boiled for a time, all the bones will become separated as the cartilage between adjacent edges disintegrates. When the foal becomes adult, the union between the bones grows stronger and by the eighth year the skull is solid and unyielding.

The two halves of the lower jaw become solidly united at the *mandibular symphysis* (located between the two central incisors) when a foal is only two months old − when it has only four temporary incisors in each jaw. Until then the two halves are separate. In the same vein, most long bones in the limbs carry articular portions (*epiphyses*) at their extremities which are united only by cartilage to the main shaft of the bone (*diaphysis*) in the young. The final solidification of these may not take place until the animal is approximately two years old and in many instances is not complete until four. Some horses will be seen to grow into their fifth and sixth years, indicating that bone growth and development is not complete in these animals until that time.

The skull consists of two main portions: the *cranium* and the *face*. The former encloses the brain, the latter the *oral* and *nasal cavities*. The division between the cranium and face may be indicated approximately by a transverse plane through the front border of the *orbits* (Fig. 7). In addition, the tongue contains its own supporting bone, the *hyoid apparatus*, made up of jointed sections between the mandibles (Fig. 15).

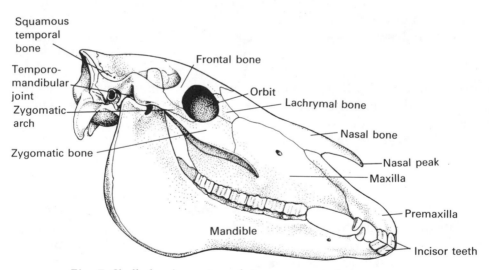

Fig. 7 Skull showing sutures between separate bones.

The Cranium

The cranium occupies the posterior third of the skull and its cavity is ovoid in shape. Its roof is formed by the upper part of the *occipital*, the *interparietal, parietal* and *frontal bones* (Fig. 9). The occipital (Fig. 10), the strongest and thickest of these, is situated at the back of the skull, of which it forms the posterior wall. It contains the *foramen magnum*, the junction of the *cranial cavity* with the *vertebral canal*, i.e. of the *brain* and *spinal cord*. On top of the occipital bone is the *nuchal crest*, the highest point of the poll, and the place most likely to be struck when a horse rears and falls backwards. However, the occipital bone itself is not so commonly fractured as the smaller bones on the floor of the cranium.

Although the other bones of the *cranial roof* are thinner than the occipital, the brain is protected at the front by the *frontal sinuses*, which provide a double roof of thin bone with a sizeable air space between them (Fig. 10). The most direct approach to the brain lies behind these sinuses, in the triangle formed between the two *temporal fossae* (Fig. 8) — the depressions immediately behind each eye — and a point level

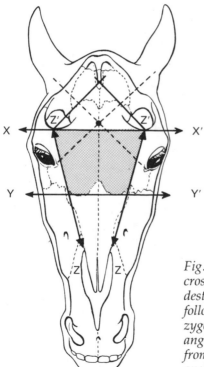

Fig. 8 Skull showing position of frontal sinuses. The crossed dotted lines mark the point of humane destruction. The sinuses can be mapped by the following axes: X—X' through the middle of the zygomatic arches; Y—Y' halfway between the inner angle of the eye and the end of the facial crest; Z—Z' from the nasomaxillary notch back through the inner angle of the eye.

with the base of each ear where the skin beneath the forelock ends on the upper limit of the forehead. Beneath this area only a relatively thin layer of bone and muscle protects the *cerebrum*, the biggest segment of the brain. This is the site of choice for humane destruction of the horse.

   Inside the skull the cranial cavity is partially divided into two compartments (Fig. 10). The anterior, larger section contains the cerebrum while the posterior section holds the *cerebellum*, an important centre in the maintenance of balance (Fig. 48). Underlying the cerebellum is the *medulla oblongata*, the link between brain and spinal cord at the *foramen magnum*.

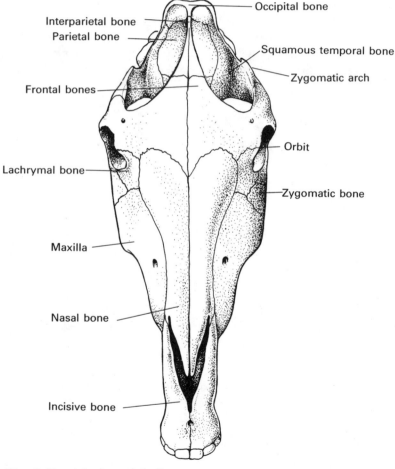

Occipital bone
Interparietal bone
Parietal bone
Squamous temporal bone
Zygomatic arch
Frontal bones
Orbit
Lachrymal bone
Zygomatic bone
Maxilla
Nasal bone
Incisive bone

Fig. 9 Frontal view of skull.

On the outer surface of the anterior part of the cranium on either side is the orbit (Fig. 9), in which is contained the eye together with a quantity of semi-fluid fat in which the eyeball is cradled. The orbit consists of a complete and prominent rim of bone which is closed by means of the *supraorbital process*, a bony arch that stretches across the orbital space from the frontal bone in the cranial roof to the *zygomatic bone* laterally. The supraorbital process can be located lying beneath the skin above the upper eyelid. This process is continuous below with a curved bar of bone known as the *zygomatic arch* which joins the *maxilla* in the lateral wall of the face and behind with the *squamous temporal bone* in the lateral wall of the cranium (Fig. 9).

Between the arch and the lower part of the cranial wall is a space in the fleshless skull continuous with the space containing the eye (Fig. 11). This space is known as the *temporal fossa* and it houses the *coronoid process* (the upper extremity) of the lower jaw. It can be seen in the living animal immediately behind the supraorbital process and is particularly noticeable during feeding, when the jaw movements force fat from the *orbital cavity* into the *fossa* as the mouth closes. This fossa is comparatively small, admitting only the tip of one finger, whereas in the dog, and other animals, it is much greater.

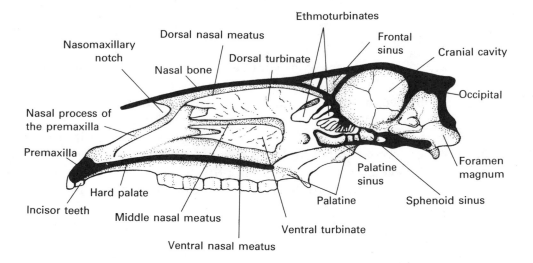

Fig. 10 Skull in sagittal section showing the interior of the nasal and cranial cavities.

The Face

The facial part of the skull overlies the nasal and oral cavities. The nasal cavity provides a passageway for respiratory airflow, and contains the sensory nerve endings involved in the sense of smell. The oral cavity lies between the upper and lower jaws. The nasal cavity lies in front of the cranial cavity separated from it by a transverse plate of bone (Fig. 10). It is divided into right and left halves by a midline, cartilaginous, *nasal septum* which passes longitudinally down the entire cavity of the nose. The *olfactory sense* is restricted to the nasal *mucous membrane* covering a series of bony projections in the hindmost part of the nasal chamber, the *ethmoid bones*. Projecting into the front part from both sides are the *turbinate bones* (also called *conchae*), providing an increased surface area for support of the highly *vascular* mucous membrane of the nose (Figs. 10 and 48). Air circulating through the spaces between the turbinates is warmed and moistened before entering the lower respiratory passages, a function that has special significance in infectious disease resistance. Notice the considerable space between the pointed peak of the nasal bones — at the *nasomaxillary notch* (Fig. 13) — and the portion of the upper jaw beneath it. Observe the amount of room taken by the nasal passages themselves.

The Sinuses

As already suggested, the comparatively large size of the skull was dictated by the animal's required powers of mastication to enable it to survive. It needed strong, continuously growing cheek teeth, and large powerful jaws, in contrast to the small cranium and light superstructures above. So the upper part of the skull was obliged to develop in a way that provided accommodation for this eating apparatus. This could have been achieved by merely increasing the surface area by new bone deposition. However this would have increased the weight of the head too much. Therefore evolution enlarged the bones by including air cavities within them; thus surface area was increased without any great increase in volume, or weight, of the whole.

There are a number of *sinuses* in each half of the head, namely the *frontal*, *superior* and *inferior maxillary*, and *sphenopalatine sinuses*. The size and position of these can best be judged by reference to Figs. 8

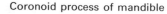

Coronoid process of mandible

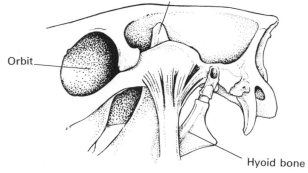

Orbit

Hyoid bone

Fig. 11 Detail of temporal area.

and 10. Briefly the frontal sinus is a large air space extending from the upper part of the nasal bones back to the level of the hind edge of the supraorbital process. The two halves, one on each side of the midline of the head, are completely separated by a thin bony partition. Each half communicates freely below with the large superior maxillary sinus of the same side, extending beneath the orbit and along the area occupied by the molar teeth. The roots of the last three cheek teeth are lodged in this sinus covered with a thin layer of bone. The inferior maxillary sinus is smaller and completely separated from the superior sinus by a thin plate of bone, but both sinuses communicate directly with the nasal passage. The remaining sinus, the sphenopalatine, is small but important. It lies below the ethmoid bones and is divided into a *posterior sphenoidal* and an *anterior palatine* part. The latter opens into the superior maxillary sinus. Infections of the first three sinuses may easily be drained by *trephining* (removing a small circular section of bone). The sphenoidal part of the sphenopalatine sinus, having something of a blind end, is liable to retain infection as it is not easily accessible to surgical interference.

The sinuses either fill, or change part of their air content during expiration. They are lined by a continuation of the mucous membrane of the nose and are readily involved in the course of nasal infections. In the horse at least they have no recognised function other than to provide the head with size and contour. They are not concerned with the sense of smell, the smell buds being confined to the *mucosa* covering the ethmoid bones.

An advantage gained from possession of the frontal and superior maxillary sinuses is that, owing to their position, they push the orbits away from the central line of the head. Thus, instead of possessing central vision with both eyes converging upon an object ahead, the eyes are placed somewhat laterally. In consequence the animal can see two objects simultaneously, one with each eye; it can also see objects approaching from behind. Although these abilities may be less useful in domestication, there is little doubt they were of considerable advantage when the horse was hunted on open grassland by preying carnivorous animals.

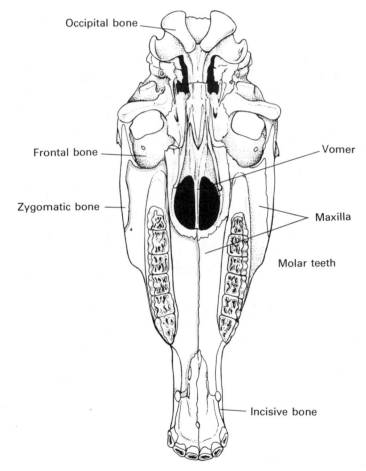

Fig. 12 Ventral view of skull.

Returning again to the facial part of the skull and in particular to the jaws; the upper jaw consists of the *maxilla* and *premaxilla*, the former housing the upper cheek teeth, the latter supporting the upper incisors (Fig. 10 and 12). Both bones help to form the walls of the nasal cavity, and meet their fellows of the opposite side in the roof of the mouth where they form the *hard palate*. The *mandible* (lower jaw, Fig. 7) is a very large structure housing the lower incisors and molars. The articulation between upper and lower jaws (*temporomandibular joint*) is seated beneath the posterior end of the zygomatic arch, as mentioned before (Fig. 11).

Below and in front of the orbit the zygomatic arch is continued forwards onto the *maxillary surface* as the *zygomatic ridge* or *facial crest*. This is designed to extend the area of origin of the powerful *masseter muscle* (the most important muscle employed in mastication), which is inserted into the flat roughened area on the outer face of the lower jaw. The other major masticatory muscle is the *temporal muscle* which extends from the upper surface of the cranium down into the *temporal fossa* to attach to the large *coronoid process* of the *mandible*.

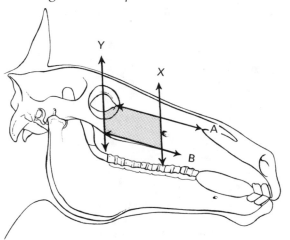

Fig. 13 Skull in lateral view showing the position of the maxillary sinus. The sinus can be mapped by the following axes: X, vertically through the facial crest close to its front end; Y, vertically through the centre of the eye; A, from the nasomaxillary notch back through the inner angle of the eye; B, along the length of the facial crest, however, this lower limit varies with age and the degree of extrusion of the teeth.

The outer surface of the skull exhibits a number of small apertures (*foramina*) through which blood vessels and nerves pass. One large *foramen* in the maxillary bone is the *infraorbital foramen*, through which passes the large, sensory, *infraorbital nerve* to the nostrils and upper lip. A further foramen, the *supraorbital foramen*, is smaller and perforates the supraorbital process of the frontal bone above the eye. It also transmits a sensory nerve to the skin covering the forehead.

The Teeth and Dentition

Examination of the teeth up to a certain period of life is one of the best methods of determining age. In the adult the permanent set consists of three *incisors*, one *canine*, three *premolars* and three *molars*, on either side of each upper and lower jaw. The *deciduous* or milk teeth are smaller and fewer in number, the adult molars having no deciduous precursors.

At birth the foal carries three cheek teeth, all temporary premolars — which later will be cast and replaced by permanent molars — and the central incisor teeth. At one year old it has four cheek teeth i.e. three

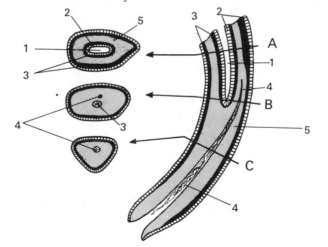

Fig. 14 Incisor tooth in long section and in cross section at the three levels A, B and C. These sections show how the shape of the tooth varies as it approaches the root, and also how the structure of the tooth table changes in accordance with the stage of wear of the crown.
(1) Infundibulum.   (2) Cement.   (3) Enamel.   (4) Pulp cavity containing new dentine.   (5) Dentine.

premolars and the first permanent molar, and a full complement of decidious incisors. At 4—5 years old it will have all six cheek teeth — the three permanent premolars and three permanent molars — and the decidious incisors will have been replaced by permanent teeth. The ages at which the incisors appear and are fully developed in each jaw may be best shown as follows:

Central incisors	*Lateral incisors*	*Corner incisors*
Cut from 2½ years,	Cut from 3½ years,	Cut from 4½ years
up to 3 years	up to 4 years	up to 5 years

A supernumerary premolar, the so-called *wolf tooth*, may appear in front of the first premolar as early as 5—6 months in the upper jaw, but usually later. The *tushes* or canine teeth are usually present in the male though small rudimentary tushes are quite common in mares. They appear at 3½—4 years and are fully developed at 4½—5 years, being absent in two-year-olds.

From five years onwards age may be determined by the shape of the masticatory surfaces of the incisor teeth and by the amount of wear shown by the depth and appearance of the *grooves* which appear on their *tables*. Teeth wear down from *crown* to *root*; at the same time they are being pushed out of the *alveolus* (socket) by growth of the root. An outer *enamel* layer covers a layer of *dentine* and also lines the central depression (*infundibulum*). As wear takes place the enamel is presented on the tooth table in a definite pattern (Fig. 14).

At six years, in a well-formed mouth, the upper and lower incisors meet in a straight line with no forward inclination. After this they commence to incline forward until at 20 years they meet at an acute angle.

Notches make their appearance in the outer edges of the upper incisors at certain ages. A notch appears at the posterior angle of the biting surface of the corner incisor at seven years. It disappears soon after eight years, and reappears at 11 years to persist sometimes throughout life. At 10 years *Galvayne's groove*, a longitudinal furrow often darkly stained, first appears at the outer portion of each upper corner incisor adjacent to the gum. By 15 years it has reached halfway down the tooth and attained its lower edge by 20 years. After this it starts to disappear from above downwards at the same rate at which it made its appearance.

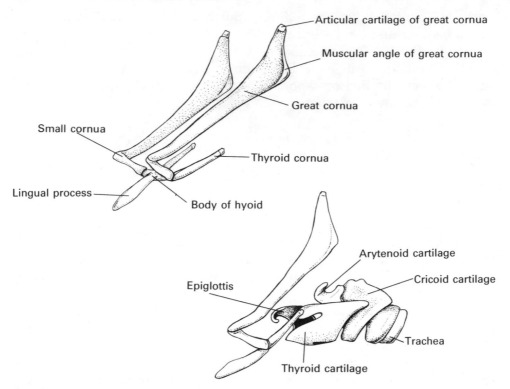

Articular cartilage of great cornua

Muscular angle of great cornua

Great cornua

Small cornua

Thyroid cornua

Lingual process

Body of hyoid

Epiglottis

Arytenoid cartilage

Cricoid cartilage

Trachea

Thyroid cartilage

Fig. 15 The hyoid apparatus and its relation to the larynx.

Before leaving the skull, attention must be given to the *hyoid apparatus* at the base of the tongue (Fig. 15). This consists of a pair of *great cornua* connected above with the *hyoid processes of the petrous temporal bones* on the underside of the skull. Below, the great cornua are attached to the transversely oriented *hyoid body* through the *small cornua*. The whole apparatus resembles a child's swing with the body of the hyoid being the seat. The body is also joined up with the *thyroid cartilage* of the *larynx* through the medium of the *thyroid cornua*. The *lingual process* projects forwards from the hyoid body and is buried in the root of the tongue. The hyoid apparatus therefore serves as an important area of attachment of tongue, pharyngeal and laryngeal muscles, and also serves to suspend the larynx in the ventral part of the throat.

3 The Spinal Column

The spine or *vertebral column* is the bony skeleton of the neck, withers, back and tail. It contains the nervous continuation of the brain, the spinal cord, and consists of seven *cervical vertebrae*; 18 *thoracic vertebrae*, each of which gives support to a pair of ribs; six *lumbar vertebrae*; a *sacrum*, made up of five bones fused by ossification of foetal cartilage; and approximately 18 *coccygeal vertebrae* (Chart 1). All these bones have a common structural plan, being built from three basic components: a *body*, an *arch*, and *processes* — each of which have different importance in the various parts of the spine.

The Cervical Vertebrae

The first two neck bones (Fig. 16) are structurally different from the others, and also from each other. The *vertebral canal*, through which the spinal cord passes, is of greater diameter in these than in other vertebrae, a precaution against damage to the cord in an area subject to a great deal of movement. The first cervical bone, the *atlas*, lacks a body which is present in all others, being a ring or short tube carrying on either side a considerable plate of bone termed the *wing*. The whole vertebra is arranged somewhat after the manner of a tortoise shell. Two large concave articular facets are present on the front for receiving the *occipital condyles* of the skull.

The second bone, the *axis*, has two peculiarities. Firstly it bears at the front of its body a tooth-like projection, the *odontoid process*, which extends forwards into the lower part of the ring formed by the atlas. The upper surface of the odontoid process is roughened to provide attachment for a strong transverse ligament which unites it to the atlas and keeps the process securely retained within the lower part of the ring of that bone. The process has articular facets to each side, and

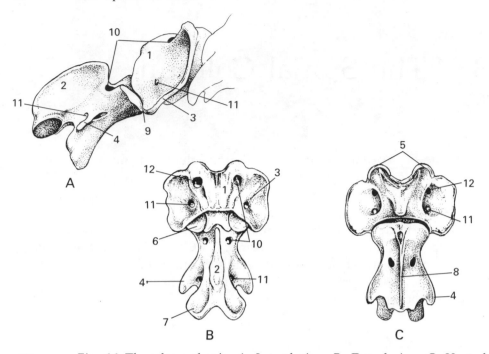

Fig. 16 The atlas and axis. A. Lateral view. B. Dorsal view. C. Ventral view.

(1) Dorsal arch of the atlas. (2) Spinous process of the axis. (3) Wing of the atlas. (4) Transverse process of the axis. (5) Anterior articular cavities of the atlas. (6) Anterior articular process of the axis. (7) Posterior articular process of the axis. (8) Ventral spine of the axis. (9) Odontoid process of the axis. (10) Intervertebral foramina. (11) Transverse foramina. (12) Alar foramen.

another below, which form joints with the hind end of the atlas. The second peculiarity is that it carries a massive and strong *dorsal spinous process*. This is thickened and divided longitudinally along its upper edge into two ridges which diverge posteriorly. Dorsal neck musculature attaches here but, more importantly, attachment is given to a portion of the *ligamentum nuchae*, the strong central ligament of the neck (Fig. 17).

The ligamentum nuchae is made of two parts.

a. A rope-like *funicular portion* which passes forwards from the highest dorsal spines of the withers over the top of the spinous process of the axis to become finally attached to the nuchal crest of the occipital bone of the skull.

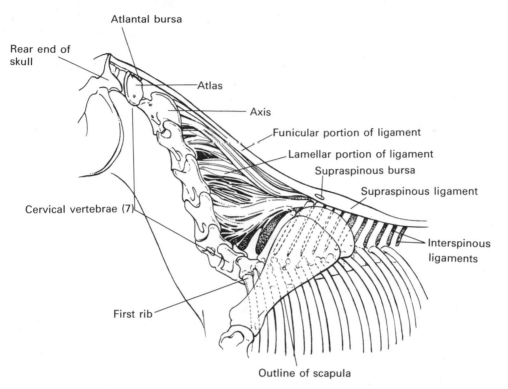

Atlantal bursa

Rear end of
skull

Atlas

Axis

Funicular portion of ligament

Lamellar portion of ligament

Supraspinous bursa

Supraspinous ligament

Cervical vertebrae (7)

Interspinous
ligaments

First rib

Outline of scapula

Fig. 17 Ligamentum nuchae.

b. A *lamellar portion* which lies in the middle of the neck and
throws out branches in fan-like formation. These are attached
at their upper ends to the underside of the funicular portion
and insert onto the dorsal surface of the middle five cervical
vertebrae below.

The ligamentum nuchae supports the position of the head and neck,
and, being elastic, also permits the head to be influenced by gravity as
well as being raised and lowered by means of the neck muscles. The
funicular portion is best viewed as a continuation forward of the
supraspinous ligament which extends along the back from the sacrum.
This attaches to the tops of all the spinous processes of lumbar and
thoracic vertebrae en route and its function is to bind these bones
together.

Two *synovial bursae* are associated with the funicular part: the *atlantal bursa* lies between the ligament and the arch of the atlas; and the *supraspinous bursa* lies over the second thoracic spine at the withers (Fig. 17). These bursae are sacs containing synovial fluid which are interposed at points of unusual pressure between a tendon, ligament or muscle and some underlying structure, usually a skeletal prominence. They facilitate ligament movement and provide some measure of protection through their cushioning effect.

The remaining five cervical vertebrae conform more to the normal vertebral plan having a body surmounted by an arch which surrounds the vertebral canal. The arch supports a low dorsal spinous process and a pair of articular processes both fore and aft. Of particular interest are the *transverse processes* which are prominent and plate-like. These project laterally and have thickened roughened edges which serve for muscle attachment, in particular the cervical part of the serratus ventralis muscle (Fig. 52). In a horse in good condition the lateral surfaces of these transverse processes can be palpated deeply through the overlying musculature on the side of the neck. Care should always be taken in giving injections here to avoid making contact with the bone.

Head Movements

The joint between the occipital bone of the skull and the atlas permits nodding (up and down) movements of the head upon the neck. The joint between the atlas and axis permits, within limits, rotation of the head on the neck, i.e. the atlas carrying the skull pivots on the odontoid process through a longitudinal axis. The joints between the last five cervical vertebrae allow lateral curvature of the neck, together with some degree of arching in which convexity of the spinal bones is directed upwards. Movements to produce the opposite condition in which the convexity is increased in a downward direction is only very limited.

The Thoracic Vertebrae

The thoracic vertebrae demonstrate the typical manner in which neighbouring spinal bones are linked together. In addition to the common articular facets, however, they possess articular surfaces to accommodate the heads of the ribs. The vertebral bodies are short when compared to those in the neck, but like them are united by intervertebral cartilage, the so-called *vertebral discs*.

At each side of the articular end of the body, before and behind, is a little concave articular surface termed the *costal facet* (Fig. 18). Through these, between each pair of vertebrae, there is created, on either side, a cup-shaped cavity for articulation with the head (*capitulum*) of a rib. Transverse processes project from the vertebral arch on either side each carrying a smooth articular surface which articulates with the *tubercle* of the rib (Fig. 20c).

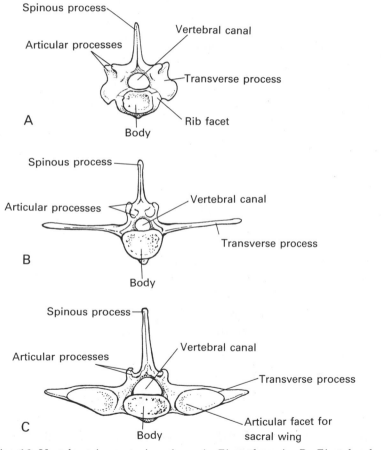

Fig. 18 Vertebrae in posterior view. A. First thoracic. B. First lumbar. C. Last lumbar.

The common *articular processes* are smaller than in the cervical region: the paired *anterior processes* articulate with the paired *posterior processes* of the adjacent vertebra.

The thoracic *spinous processes* are of great size in the early vertebrae reaching their maximum height at the fourth and diminishing to the fifteenth or sixteenth (the *anticlinal* or *diaphragmatic vertebra*). The first fifteen spines point backwards, the anticlinal vertebra is vertical, the last two incline forwards (Chart 1). Out of the 18 thoracic bones the first seven lie partly behind the sloping *scapula*, which also covers the heads of the third to seventh ribs. There is very limited movement in the thoracic part of the spine of the horse in any direction.

The Lumbar Vertebrae

There are usually six lumbar bones, but occasionally only five are present. In the latter case, an extra thoracic vertebra occurs and is found especially in eastern breeds such as the Arab. The lumbar vertebrae are remarkable for the length and width of their transverse processes which project at almost right angles from their bodies (Fig. 18). Each may be 7–10 cm (2.8–4 in) in length and 2 cm (0.8 in) in width. The lumbar vertebrae of the horse differ from those of other animals since the lateral processes of the last three carry extra articular facets, one on each side of the cartilage that joins the bodies together. These facets are present only on the hinder edge in the case of the fourth lumbar, but they are also present on the leading edge of the first of the fused sacral bones (Fig. 19). This ensures that the last three lumbar vertebrae and the sacrum are united by true synovial joints on their transverse processes and by cartilage joining together their bodies. This means that in the region of the loins the vertebral column has a strictly defined and very limited degree of movement.

The Sacrum

This composite bone, lying beneath the loins in the region of the croup, is composed of five vertebrae fused firmly together (Fig. 19). Sometimes the first of the coccygeal vertebrae will be found solidly fused to the sacrum giving the impression that it contains six bones instead of five. The sacrum is triangular in form and lies in the roof of

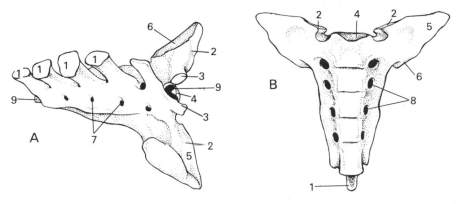

Fig. 19 The sacrum showing the five fused vertebrae. A. Dorsolateral view. B. Ventral view.
(1) Spinous processes.   (2) Articular facets for articulation with the last lumbar vertebra.   (3) Articular processes.   (4) Body.   (5) Sacral wing.
(6) Auricular surface which forms sacroiliac joint.   (7) Dorsal sacral foramina.
(8) Ventral sacral foramina.   (9) Sacral part of vertebral canal.

the pelvic cavity with its posterior a little higher than its anterior end.

The pelvic bones representing − through the *ilia* − the upper extremity of the hind limbs, are united to the sacrum on either side at their somewhat roughened *auricular surfaces*. These are not joined by typical synovial joints but by means of an interosseous ligament composed of short, strong, white fibres, the *sacroiliac ligament*, which divides the articulation up into a series of small synovial joints.

The Coccygeal Vertebrae

There are usually 18 coccygeal, or tail, bones, perhaps one more or less at times, which follow the sacrum. These begin to lose their articular processes and their central canals after the third vertebra, until the terminal bones become merely short, solid rods united by discs of cartilage.

The Vertebral Column as a Whole

The total outline of the spine presents a succession of curves when viewed from the side (Chart 1). It is slightly arched (concave below) at the upper end of the neck, but becomes concave above in the lower third of the neck before joining the thoracic section. At the junction of the neck and thorax there is a marked change in direction and a very gentle curve, concave below, extends throughout the thoracic and lumbar regions. It should be noticed that a line drawn through the summits of the spinous processes does not correspond to the curves formed by the vertebral bodies — because these processes are varied in length.

The slight ventrally concave bow of the thoracolumbar region provides a static advantage in supporting the body weight. If the column were straight, or convex beneath, this weight acting downwards would tend to decrease the area of contact between adjacent vertebral bodies, whereas with ventral concavity, body weight tends to increase it. The dorsal spines of the thorax are bound in a row by strong ligaments and each neighbouring pair is firmly united through the articular processes aided by a number of closely binding ligaments — making them into an almost rigid column.

Spinal Movement

The spine of the horse exhibits only limited movement except at neck and tail. The movement that does occur in the thoracolumbar region is found between individual thoracic vertebrae, between the last thoracic and first lumbar, between the first three lumbar, and at the lumbosacral junction. As said earlier, the total lateral deviation has been estimated in the region of 15–20 cm (6–8 in) for the full length of the fixed part of the spine. This movement is necessarily dependent to a great extent upon the thickness of the intervertebral discs, which are firmly united to the bodies of the vertebrae — so much so that one might regard intervertebral cartilages as portions of the bodies which have not yet become calcified. With advanced years calcification is common and very frequently further outgrowths of bone act as bridges between bones making union almost complete.

In the synovial articulations between the transverse processes of the last three lumbar vertebrae, an active arthritis may occur as early as the second or third year in one or more vertebrae, terminating in solid fusion, often with the formation of fresh bony deposits surrounding the actual joints. The lumbosacral joint is not normally included in this

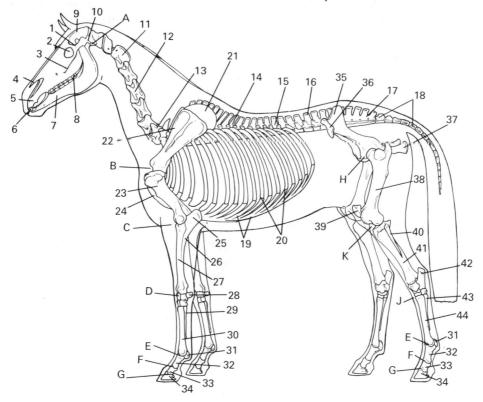

Chart 1 The bones of the horse.
(1) Supraorbital process.   (2) Orbit.   (3) Facial crest.   (4) Nasal peak.
(5) Pre-maxilla.   (6) Incisor teeth.   (7) Lower jaw.   (8) Cheek teeth (molars
and premolars).   (9) Nuchal crest.   (10) Atlas.   (11) Axis.   (12) Fourth
cervical vertebra.   (13) Seventh cervical vertebra.   (14) Ninth thoracic
vertebra.   (15) Last thoracic vertebra.   (16) Fourth lumbar vertebra.
(17) Sacrum.   (18) Coccygeal vertebrae.   (19) Costal cartilages. (20) Ribs.
(21) Cartilage of prolongation of scapula.   (22) Scapula.   (23) Humerus.
(24) Sternum.   (25) Olecranon process.   (26) Ulna.   (27) Radius.
(28) Accessory carpal.   (29) Small metacarpal.   (30) Large metacarpal.
(31) Proximal sesamoid.   (32) First phalanx.   (33) Second phalanx.
(34) Third phalanx.   (35) Tuber sacrale.   (36) Tuber coxae.   (37) Tuber
ischii.   (38) Femur.   (39) Patella.   (40) Fibula.   (41) Tibia.   (42) Tuber
calcis.   (43) Small metatarsal.   (44) Large metatarsal.   (A) Jaw or
temporomandibular joint.   (B) Shoulder joint.   (C) Elbow joint.   (D) Knee
joint.   (E) Fetlock joint.   (F) Pastern joint.   (G) Coffin joint.   (H) Hip
joint.   (J) Hock joint.   (K) Stifle joint.

process — known as *ankylosis*. Examination of the skeleton of horses of all ages indicates that fusion is the rule rather than the exception. Unfortunately, however, the extent of this and its rate of progress is not always general, so that two adjacent lumbar vertebrae may be united on one side and unattached on the other. This condition may be conducive to pain and impaired efficiency in horses expected to race, hunt or jump. However, many of these cases recover when fusion finally takes place.

The vertebral column, being the axis upon which the limbs act to produce movement, is flexed in the thoracolumbar area by forces produced by pushing back the hind limbs against the ground. Both oblique and vertical forces are exerted on the spine by the hind limbs. Oblique forces are exhibited as a tendency to flex the spine sideways, while vertical forces tend to increase the curvature of the thoracolumbar bow, i.e. to flex it vertically. Sideways forces and the resultant lateral oscillation are clearly apparent at the walk. At speeds higher than that, however, muscular resistance makes the column as rigid as possible in order to eliminate sideways movement.

Vertical forces tending to increase the curvature of the spine are also resisted and straightening of the thoracolumbar bow adds significantly to the forward propulsive thrust. Above the spinal column the *longissimus dorsi* muscle and below it the *psoas minor* muscle cooperate by simultaneous contraction in an effort to counter attempts to flex the spine. When the synchronisation between these muscles fails, as during a fall or even galloping on level ground — and sometimes during anaesthesia — fracture of the back may occur. The damage usually takes place in the thoracic region.

The calibre of the vertebral canal, through which the spinal cord passes releasing nerve trunks back along the body, varies in different regions. This is designed to give the cord full protection. The calibre is greatest at the atlas, the first cervical vertebra, but it diminishes considerably until the last three cervical and first two thoracic vertebrae where it becomes a great deal larger to accommodate the cervical enlargement of the cord. After this it narrows again until it reaches its minimum size in the middle of the back. It increases again at the lumbar enlargement, until the last or second last lumbar bone, when it diminishes until the canal disappears fully at about the fourth coccygeal vertebra. The spinal cord actually comes to an end in the middle of the

sacrum giving off coccygeal nerves which extend back in the spinal
canal and supply the tail.

The Ribs

There are normally eighteen pairs of ribs, each thoracic vertebrae carying a rib on either side − or one pair of ribs fits its heads
between each pair of thoracic bones (Fig. 20).

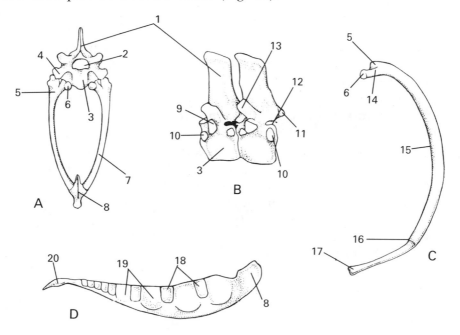

*Fig. 20 Thoracic rib-cage components. A. First thoracic vertebra with
first ribs, anterior view. B. Fifteenth and sixteenth thoracic vertebrae,
lateral view. C. Eighth rib, anterior view. D. Sternum showing its
segmented nature, lateral view.*

*(1) Spinous processes. (2) Vertebral canal. (3) Body. (4) Transverse process.
(5) Tubercle of rib. (6) Head (capitulum) of rib. (7) First rib. (8) Cariniform
cartilage of sternum. (9) Tubercular facet. (10) Capitular facet.
(11) Articular process. (12) Intervertebral foramen. (13) Mamillary process.
(14) Neck of rib. (15) Eighth rib. (16) Costochondral junction. (17) Costal
cartilage. (18) Costal facets. (19) Sternebrae. (20) Xiphoid cartilage.*

A rib is an elongated, curved and highly elastic bone. At its lower end it carries a prolongation in the form of a rod of cartilage − the *costal cartilage*. The first eight pairs articulate through their costal cartilages with the sides of the *sternum*, i.e. the breastbone, and are termed *sternal ribs*. The last ten pairs do not do this; these *asternal ribs* have their cartilaginous prolongations bound together, each being attached for nearly its whole length to its predecessor in the series forming the *costal arch* (Chart 1). In young horses the rib cartilages are soft and gristly in nature, but in old animals they become calcified and solid. The first rib (Fig. 20a) is short and the least curved. The degree of curvature increases up to the last rib, the cartilage of which is not attached to the one in front of it, but projects freely into the abdominal wall. This last rib is short and termed the *floating rib*.

Between and overlying the ribs are muscles which cause them to rotate in a forward and outward direction to induce inspiration (Chart 3). Owing to the curvature of the ribs, the chest capacity is thus increased and inspiration occurs as air is drawn into the lungs. When the ribs rotate in the opposite direction to lie flat against the chest wall air is expelled from the lungs. Between the serous membrane (*parietal pleura*) lining the inside of the chest wall and that covering the lungs (*visceral pleura*), there is a potential cavity containing a vacuum. The two layers of pleura are kept in close apposition by a thin fluid film allowing the lungs to dilate and contract in accordance with the movements of the chest wall.

The first rib, although the smallest, is especially important since it carries on its anterior edge grooves which are imprints of the nerves of the *brachial plexus*, a collection of large nerve trunks which supply locomotory and sensory impulses to the forelimb. If this rib is injured during accidents or falls, the resulting swelling may put pressure on some of these nerves causing muscular paralysis and skin desensitisation. The commonest type of damage is radial paralysis, the radial being the nerve supplying the extensor muscles below the shoulder. In this situation the horse cannot bring the lower part of the limb forward and so the knee remains flexed and the foot drags along the ground at the toe. At the same time the elbow, lacking muscular support, drops below its normal position; because of this, radial paralysis is often termed *dropped elbow*.

One other important factor concerning the ribs is that the lateral surfaces of the first nine give origin to the thoracic part of the *serratus ventralis* muscle (Fig. 52). The cervical part of this muscle originates from the transverse processes of the last five cervical vertebrae. The two parts together form a large muscular fan on the lateral surface of the thorax and neck which converges dorsally onto the inner face of the scapula. The significance of this will become apparent later.

The Sternum

The sternum forms the floor of the thorax or chest, and is held in position by the first eight pairs of ribs, the lower ends of which join up with it on either side at regular intervals by means of their costal cartilages (Fig. 20). The sternum is long, narrow and canoe-shaped but is not actually a single bone. It is made up of a number of distinct bony segments connected by intervening cartilage in the young horse; a great deal of this remaining throughout life. The sternum and costal cartilages give extensive origin to the *pectoral* muscles which pass outwards to attachment areas on the fascia of the arm and shaft of the humerus. One important muscle, the *anterior deep pectoral*, passes up around the front of the shoulder to an insertion on the *prescapular fascia*. Like the serratus ventralis, its importance will be explained later.

In front, the sternum carries the *presternal* or *cariniform* cartilage which gives attachment to some of the neck muscles, e.g. the *sternomandibularis* which forms the lower border of the jugular furrow and attaches to the *mandibular ramus* of the lower jaw. The hinder end of the sternum is drawn out into a flat, heart-shaped *xiphoid* cartilage which forms the floor at the front end of the abdomen and gives attachment to the sternal fibres of the diaphragm, the muscular partition between thorax and abdomen. The remainder of the diaphragmatic musculature arises from the costal arch and the undersides of the lumbar vertebrae.

4   The Forelimb

The important thing to remember about the forelimb is that it is not attached to the body by bone, nor by anything firmer and harder than muscle and ligamentous material. The horse has no *clavicle* (collar bone) and it is possible to dissect the forelimb from the carcass using only a knife. One advantage of this structuring is that the muscles holding limb and body together, plus the extensor and flexor muscles within the limb, are able to absorb a great deal of concussive force that is transmitted upwards, and which would go to the spine if this were more solidly united to the body.

From above to below, the bones of the forelimb are:

a. The *scapula*, which extends from the withers to the shoulder joint.
b. The *humerus*, reaching from shoulder to elbow.
c. The *radius* and *ulna*, extending from elbow to knee (these two bones are fused together in the horse).
d. The *carpus*, or knee, made up of seven bones most of which are flattened and fitted with wide, smooth articular surfaces.
e. The *metacarpal bones*, only one of which is fully functional (the small metacarpals on either side merely help to support some of the knee bones and represent the remains of two other digits possessed by horses in the past).
f. The *phalanges*, of which there are three in the modern soliped horse:
   (i)   the single, undivided *first phalanx* (long pastern bone);
   (ii) the shorter *second phalanx* (short pastern bone) lying partly inside the hoof and partly above it at the coronet;
   (iii) the *third phalanx* (pedal bone) lying entirely within the hoof.

g. The *sesamoid bones*, being two *proximal* sesamoids at the back of the fetlock and the *distal* sesamoid at the back of the third phalanx.

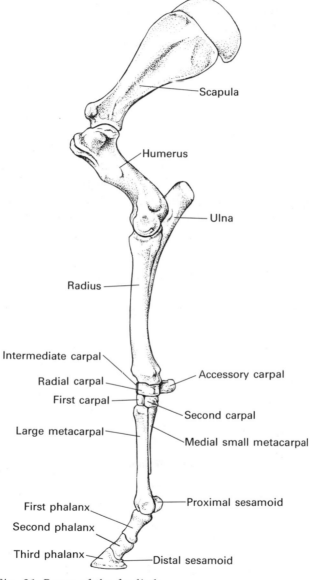

Fig. 21 Bones of the forelimb

The Scapula

This bone is a triangular, flattened plate (Fig. 22) attaching the forelimb to the trunk by means of muscles and ligaments. It partially covers, from the lateral aspect, the first six or seven ribs, from which it is separated by muscles underlying it and also by loose connective tissue. This connective tissue permits the scapula to move freely over the ribs when pulled by muscles attached to its surfaces and borders.

The thorax is actually slung up between the two scapulae through the serratus ventralis muscles, one on either side. This means that just as the scapulae can glide upon the ribs so the trunk can move about between the scapulae (Fig. 2). This degree of movement is brought about by unilateral contraction of the *serratus ventralis, anterior deep pectoral, rhomboideus* and *trapezius* muscles, all having attachments to the scapulae. Weight is shifted to the limb on the acting side, and this is of great importance in maintaining balance especially when cornering at speed and moving over uneven ground. It is this mechanism which enables a polo pony or cutting horse to carry out bending movements at speed.

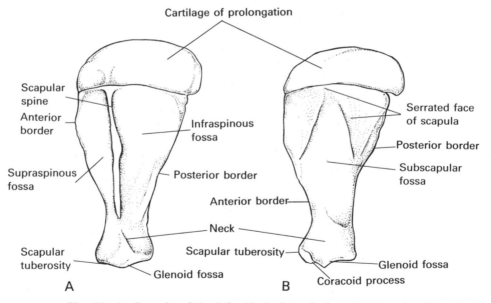

Fig. 22 A. Scapula of the left side in lateral view. B. Scapula of the right side in medial view.

The freedom of movement attained by slinging the thorax like this has been a significant factor in the evolution of the modern horse. Indeed it made it a match, in the wild, for the carnivorous animals which possess flexible spines and are able to develop great speed over short distances (Fig. 1).

The outer surface of the scapula is triangular with the base uppermost. It is divided longitudinally by a prominent ridge, the *scapular spine*, which cuts it into two sections of which the posterior is the wider. The two cavities thus formed are filled by muscle, the *supraspinatus* in front and the *infraspinatus* behind. These muscles are detectable through the skin and between them the spine of the scapula can be felt with the fingers. The supraspinatus extends the shoulder joint thus advancing the limb generally, while the infraspinatus rotates the limb in an outward direction. As well as separating these two muscles, the scapular spine provides the insertion of the trapezius muscle as this extends down over the withers from its origin in the mid-dorsal line. It also serves for the origin of the *deltoid* muscle which crosses the outer surface of the shoulder joint to attach to the humerus (Chart 3).

The inner surface of the scapula is hollowed along its length for the origin of the *subscapularis* muscle, which is an adductor of the limb, i.e. it draws the limb towards the midline and prevents it from being pulled outwards away from the body.

The upper edge of the scapula carries a crescent-shaped *cartilage of prolongation*, a part of the foetal scapula which has never undergone ossification. The inner surface of this gives attachment to the rhomboideous muscle (Fig. 52). This anchors the scapula to the *ligamentum nuchae* and the front eight or nine thoracic spines. It pulls the upper end of the scapula forwards, as well as helping to rotate the thorax between the two limbs (Fig. 2).

At its lower end the scapula tapers to a neck which carries the *glenoid cavity* for articulation with the head of the humerus. A projection known as the *scapular tuberosity* lies in front of the glenoid cavity occupying a very exposed spot close to the point of the shoulder where injury from contusion, especially among hunters and jumpers may occur. This tuberosity gives origin to the *biceps brachii* muscle which is a shoulder extensor (also an elbow flexor). Between the tendon of this muscle and the head of the humerus is the *intertuberal synovial bursa*, which protects and facilitates the movement of the biceps tendon in the *intertuberal groove*. Damage to this bursa is a common cause of shoulder lameness.

From the hindmost (or lower) edge of the scapula the long head of the triceps muscle takes its origin. This muscle, which lies beneath the front of the saddle flap in a ridden horse, inserts onto the point of the elbow and is a powerful extensor of the elbow joint, as well as having a flexing effect on the shoulder. It is a prominent landmark of the horse's shoulder region (Chart 2), and provides support at the front of the rider's shinbone. The *teres major* muscle also takes its origin from the lower border of the scapula and inserts onto the upper end of the humerus, the muscle being an important shoulder flexor.

The scapula varies in different individuals with regard to its degree of obliquity, i.e. the degree of angulation between it and the horizontal. It is preferable that this angle should be as small as possible, an upright scapula creates a straightness of the shoulder which is undesirable. The degree of inclination depends on several factors, one of these being the length of the bone itself. A long scapula must necessarily be inclined back, while a short one can stand erect. Also important is the length of the thoracic spines; the upper end of the scapula is attached to the spinal bones. When these spines are long and the bones to which the scapula is attached lie further back, the scapula must be set more obliquely. A long scapula, well inclined, enables the horse to advance the humerus much farther than when it is set in a more upright position. If the humerus can be carried farther forward it follows that the knee and foot will follow suit. This makes for free front action and a long sweeping stride such as is desired of a hack or hunter. Not only does an upright scapula spoil the shape of the withers and the set-on of the neck, it also shortens the forward stride by moving through a much narrower angle.

The Shoulder Joint

The shoulder joint is formed between the glenoid cavity of the scapula, its articular cup, and the articular head of the humerus. It is enclosed in a joint capsule which resembles a double-mouthed sac, one edge of which encircles the rim of the glenoid cavity, while the other encircles the periphery of the humeral head. In spite of its considerable surface it is the only joint in the limbs which has no definite *collateral ligaments.* The two functions of these ligaments — maintaining articular continuity and directing joint movements along habitual pathways — are replaced by numerous powerful muscles surrounding the joint. These help to hold the bones in apposition. They include the supraspinatus, infraspinatus and subscapularis already mentioned.

The Humerus

Although the humerus is one of the strongest bones in the body it is sometimes shattered during a gallop on the flat as the result of imperfect muscular synchronisation. It is positioned obliquely in the limb between the glenoid cavity of the scapula and the heads of the radius and ulna below (Fig. 21). Its upper end is large with a convex articular head which is almost circular in shape in order to fit the glenoid cavity. In front of the articular head is the well-marked *intertuberal* or *bicipital groove* between the medial and lateral tuberosities. This groove is divided by a central ridge into two channels and is

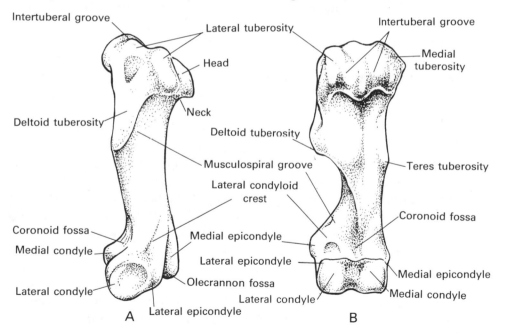

Fig. 23 A. Humerus of the left side in lateral view. B. Humerus of the right side in anterior view.

covered by thick fibrocartilage. The tendon of the biceps muscle plays over it and the fibrocartilage is modelled to correspond with the face of the tendon to enable it to glide through with ease.

A large pad of fat separates the biceps tendon from the shoulder joint capsule, and a *synovial bursa* facilitates the passage of the tendon through the groove. This bursa thus occupies a very prominent position in the forelimb and is subject to injury from direct contact with doors, rails or fence posts. Serious lameness may ensue, though it is a form of lameness that lends itself to treatment with modern methods of physiotherapy. Lameness of the shoulder joint, contrary to common belief, is not that usual, although lameness caused by injury to muscles in the region is widespread.

The *lateral tuberosity* at the upper end of the humerus is large and divided into two parts. The anterior part borders the bicipital groove and gives attachment to the lateral branch of the supraspinatus muscle; the posterior part gives attachment to the infraspinatus (Fig. 52). The *medial tuberosity* is smaller and also in two parts. The front part borders the inner side of the intertuberal groove and gives attachment to the medial branch of the supraspinatus and posterior deep pectoral muscles; the hind part gives attachment to the subscapularis.

The *shaft* of the humerus possesses a *musculospiral groove* winding around onto the front of the bone above the elbow. This lodges the *brachialis* muscle, a flexor of the elbow joint. On the outer surface of the shaft, little less than halfway down, the *deltoid tuberosity* juts out to give attachment to the deltoid muscle. This prominence can easily be palpated through the horse's skin (Chart 2) and as it is so prominent it sometimes becomes injured in collisions and may give rise to lameness. On the medial surface of the shaft, a smaller prominence, the *teres tuberosity*, provides attachment for the teres major and *latissimus dorsi* muscles, two of the main limb retractors. The humeral shaft also provides areas on its posterior surface for the origin of the shorter heads of the *triceps* muscle (the lateral and medial heads).

At its lower end the humerus has an oblique *trochlear surface* (a deep groove between two prominent smooth *condyles*) for articulation with the radius and ulna. Each condyle also supports on its lateral surface an *epicondyle* for origin of some of the flexor and extensor muscles of the forearm. The *medial epicondyle* is by far the larger and projects posteriorly behind the level of the articular surface of the elbow joint. Its importance is that it gives origin to parts of the deep and superficial digital flexor muscles which play a major role in elbow fixation — because both have tendinous components extending throughout their bellies. Other parts of these muscles originate lower down on the *olecranon process* and the surface of the radius and ulna. On the hind surface of the humerus at its lower end, a large excavation, the *olecranon fossa*, lies between the epicondyles. This fossa receives the *anconeal process* of the ulna when the elbow joint is extended.

The Radius and Ulna

The radius of the horse is larger than the ulna to which it is united by ligamentous fibres in the young animal, and by solid bone in the adult (Fig. 24). In the normal standing position the radius is held approximately vertical and the angle between the obliquely inclined humerus and the radius at the elbow is 145 degrees. There is no movement between radius and ulna in the horse — in humans the bones move freely on one another enabling the palm of the hand to be turned upwards (*supinate*) or downwards (*pronate*).

The upper end of the radius forms an articular surface in conjunction with the ulna which is moulded upon the lower articular surface of the humerus. The *radial articular surface* is bounded by a well-defined rim and its middle portion carries a raised projection, the *coronoid process*. The lateral surface of the upper end of the radius gives attachment to parts of the common and lateral extensor muscles of the digit. Carpal and digital flexor components arise from the olecranon process and the posterior surfaces of both radius and ulna. We have already seen that the bulk of the digital flexor muscles come from the medial epicondyle of the humerus, as does the bulk of the carpal flexor mass (*flexor carpi radialis*, *flexor carpi ulnaris*). However one carpal flexor, the *ulnaris lateralis*, does have an origin on the lateral epicondyle of the humerus.

The lower end of the radius is provided with a carpal articular surface carrying several facets which correspond with those of the upper row of carpal or knee bones.

Whereas in man, and most animals, the ulna is larger than the radius, in the horse it is small and short apart from its hindmost large projection, the olecranon process. This is a prominent structure projecting upward and somewhat backward behind the lower end of the

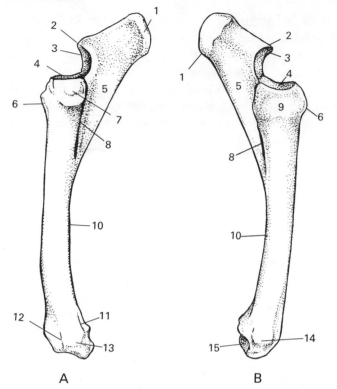

Fig. 24 Radius and ulna of the left side. A. Lateral view. B. Medial view.
(1) Olecranon process. (2) Anconeal process. (3) Semilunar notch.
(4) Humeral articular surface. (5) Shaft of the ulna. (6) Radial tuberosity.
(7) Lateral tuberosity for the attachment of extensor muscles. (8) Interosseous
space. (9) Medial tuberosity. (10) Shaft of radius. (11) Groove for lateral
extensor tendon. (12) Groove for common extensor tendon. (13) Tuberosity
for the lateral carpal ligament. (14) Tuberosity for the medial carpal ligament.
(15) Carpal articular surface.

humerus forming a lever arm for the extensor muscles (triceps) of the
elbow. It has an outer convex surface and an anterior edge terminating
in a beak-like structure, the anconeal process, which is housed in the
olecranon fossa between the epicondyles on the lower end of the
humerus when the joint is extended. The ulna is noteworthy in having
no central marrow cavity which other long bones of the limbs possess.
The body of the ulna is a triangular portion of bone with its apex at its
lowest part a little above the centre of the radius.

The Elbow Joint

The elbow (Fig. 25), like most limb joints, is a ginglymus, or hinge, joint. It acts freely in one direction, without lateral movement. However, it differs in that the position of maximum contact of the two articular surfaces is the middle position, i.e. not the flexed or extended positions as in most other limb joints. The middle position, or the position of maximum joint stability of the elbow, lies between 140 and 150 degrees dorsal angle   the normal standing angle. The elbow joint is braced in this position by its *collateral ligaments*, by muscular co-operation between the elbow flexors and extensors, and by the action of the digital flexors originating on the medial epicondyle. During elbow flexion the collateral ligaments loosen and the bones of the forearm (radius and ulna) do not move in the exact plane of the humerus, but rotate a little outwards around the anatomical axis of the radius. When this peculiarity is overpronounced the horse throws its forefoot a little outwards during elbow flexion especially when trotting. It is then said to dish.

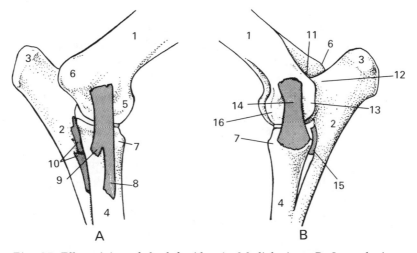

Fig. 25 Elbow joint of the left side. A. Medial view. B. Lateral view.
(1) Humerus. (2) Shaft of the ulna. (3) Olecranon process. (4) Radius.
(5) Medial condyle. (6) Medial epicondyle. (7) Radial tuberosity. (8) Long medial collateral ligament. (9) Short medial collateral ligament. (10) Medial transverse radioulnar ligament. (11) Olecranon fossa. (12) Anconeal process. (13) Lateral epicondyle. (14) Lateral collateral ligament. (15) Lateral transverse radioulnar ligament. (16) Humeral trochlea.

Owing to the passage of the anconeal process into the olecranon fossa of the humerus, aided by the strong collateral ligaments which hold radius and ulna together, and the biceps muscle and cranial ligament of the joint, overextension of the elbow is not possible. The bones of the arm and forearm cannot therefore be brought into the same straight line.

The Carpus or Knee

There are usually seven carpal bones, but sometimes eight, arranged in two rows one above the other. The bones of the upper row are: *radial carpal, intermediate carpal, ulnar carpal* and the *accessory carpal* at the back. Those of the lower row are: *first carpal, second carpal, third carpal* and *fourth carpal*. The positioning and relationships of the carpal bones will be better understood by reference to Figs. 26 and 27.

The accessory carpal is a flattened, four-sided bone which articulates with the rear of the ulnar carpal on the outer side of the back of the carpus, and the radius above. The inner surface is concave and forms, with the posterior surface of the radial and intermediate carpals, the *carpal groove*. This is converted into a *carpal canal* by deep and superficial ligaments, through which the tendons of the deep and superficial flexor muscles pass down behind the knee within the *carpal synovial sheath*. The outer surface of the accessory carpal bone carries a furrow (Fig. 27A) down which the long tendon of the *ulnaris lateralis* muscle passes. The accessory carpal does not bear weight directly, being a sesamoid bone which is interposed in the course of the tendons of the middle and lateral carpal flexors (*flexor carpi ulnaris* and *ulnaris lateralis*). It enables these to work at a mechanical advantage giving greater leverage since the bone takes on the role of a pulley block.

Movement of the Knee Joint

The carpus or knee can be considered another ginglymus joint in that it moves only in one direction, that of flexion and extension, without lateral or rotatory movements. When the knee is flexed with the foot close to the elbow, the joint can be seen to be a compound one containing three subsidiary joints. A gap forms at the front between the radius and the upper row of carpal bones (*radio-carpal joint*); a

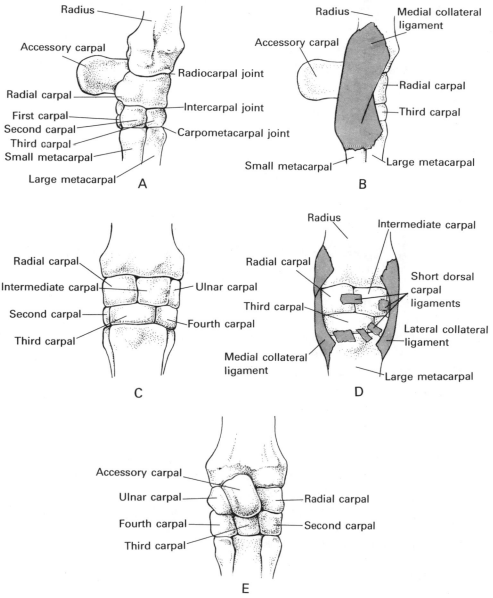

Fig. 26 Carpus of the left side. A. Medial view. B. Medial view showing the main ligaments. C. Anterior view. D. Anterior view showing the main ligaments. E. Posterior view.

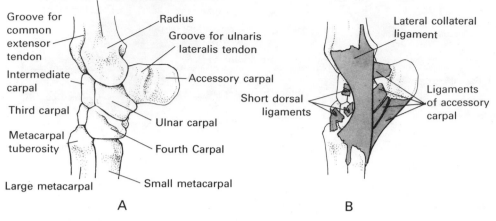

Fig. 27 Carpus of the left side. A. Lateral view. B. Lateral view showing the main ligaments.

second gap forms between the two rows of carpal bones (*intercarpal joint*). A third gap is hardly noticeable, that between the lower row of carpal bones and the *metacarpus* (*carpo-metacarpal joint*). Movement is provided for by the manner in which the carpal-connecting ligaments are arranged (Fig. 26C), and by the slackness of the *anterior carpal ligament*, which in the extended state is quite loose fitting.

During extension of the carpus, movement is arrested when the large metacarpal bone comes into line with the radius — this happens because the back of the knee is contained within a strong *posterior* or *volar carpal ligament* (the deep lining of the carpal canal), and by other ligaments between the radius and carpus, and also between the rows of carpal bones. The volar carpal ligament is continued down as the *subcarpal* or *inferior check ligament* to blend with the deep flexor tendon (Fig. 62). This structure is a part of the stay apparatus explained later.

The carpal joints are set slightly obliquely so that during knee flexion the foot turns outwards a little from the central plane of the forearm. When the knee is fully flexed the strong collateral ligaments relax sufficiently to permit slight movement of the foot outwardly and inwardly (abduction and adduction). (In cases of capped elbow it is usually the inner heel of the shoe which causes bruising by making contact with the point of the elbow while the horse is lying down.)

The tendons of the extensor muscles of the digit pass over the front of the knee enclosed in *synovial sheaths* to ensure smooth passage. A synovial sheath differs from a *bursa* in that the *synovial sac* is wrapped around a tendon. The inner layer is attached to the tendon, the outer layer, in this case, lines the carpal canal in which the tendon runs. The two layers can glide over one another freely being lubricated by the *synovial fluid* between them. These tendons can be felt with the fingers, and if their synovial sheaths become distended with fluid their positions can then be seen.

The Metacarpal Bones

There are three *metacarpal bones* two of which, together with their attendent digits, have regressed over the centuries until they serve no practical purpose now other than as support for some of the carpal bones. The digits which have undergone reduction are represented by the *small metacarpal*, or *splint, bones* − equivalent to the index and ring fingers of the human hand − while the *large metacarpal*, or *cannon, bone* is the equine equivalent of the middle finger.

The shaft of the large metacarpal (Fig. 28) is slender but capable of carrying a great deal of weight. Its strength depends upon the thickness of the solid bone surrounding the cancellous, i.e. spongy, *medullary cavity*, which is small; the metacarpal being almost completely solid bone throughout. The term 'bone' is applied by horseman and judges referring to the metacarpal region of the horse. That which is assessed and described includes the metacarpal bones, the *periosteum*, a number of tendons, blood vessels and nerves, the suspensory and check ligaments, a variable amount of connective tissue and the overlying skin. While the exercise has its limitations there is an evident difference in the external dimensions of this area from one animal to another. The size is a guide to ability to bear weight and stand up to work on hard surfaces, and it is an important aspect of judging foals and yearlings for purchase, particularly for prospective racing purposes, because light-boned types are less likely to stand up to the rigours of two-year-old racing. While bone may well be of similar durability in the laboratory, its size and strength in the living animal will help decide the type of work to which that animal will best be suited. A long narrow cannon bone is inevitably weaker than a short one of greater circumference.

About three-quarters of the upper articular surface of the large meta-carpal bone supports the third carpal. On its outer side the fourth carpal articulates, and on its inner side the second articulates. At the front of the head, immediately below the knee, is a prominence, the *metacarpal tuberosity*, onto which the tendon of the extensor *carpi radialis*

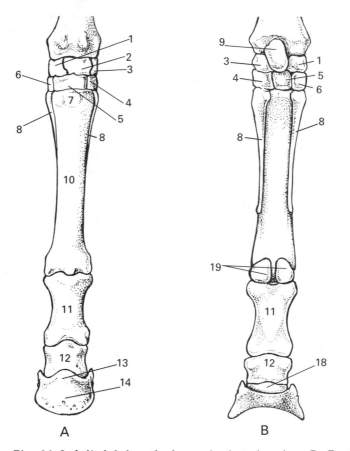

Fig. 28 Left limb below the knee. A. Anterior view. B. Posterior view.
(1) Radial carpal. (2) Intermediate carpal. (3) Ulnar carpal. (4) Fourth carpal. (5) Third carpal. (6) Second carpal. (7) Metacarpal tuberosity.
(8) Small metacarpals. (9) Accessory carpal. (10) Large metacarpal.
(11) First phalanx. (12) Second phalanx. (13) Extensor process. (14) Third phalanx. (15) Semilunar crest. (16) Solar area. (17) Flexor area.
(18) Distal sesamoid bone. (19) Proximal sesamoid bones.

muscle inserts, together with the *lacertus fibrosus* from the biceps muscle which has blended with the carpal extensor tendon. This is an important element of the *stay apparatus* (Fig. 62). At the back of the metacarpal head, and on either side, is a facet which forms a synovial joint with the appropriate small metacarpal bone. The lower end of the large metacarpal has basically two articulating areas; one for articulation below with the first phalanx, a second for articulation with the proximal sesamoid bones at its rear.

The hind surface of the large metacarpal is flat from side to side, and, with the small metacarpals, forms a wide groove which houses the suspensory ligament. Up to three or four years, the union between large and small metacarpal is fibrous and some up and down movement is transferred to the splint bones from the knee movements during locomotion. This movement, especially near the union between the bones, may set up an inflammatory reaction in the periosteal covering of both large and small metacarpals, and give rise to the condition known as splints — a frequent cause of lameness in young horses. However, it is a condition which usually improves when the bones become firmly fused either from age or post-inflammatory union brought about by the deposition of fresh bone between the large and smaller bones. Such inflammatory changes may be ascribed to: (a) heredity; (b) conformation; (c) concussion resulting from excessive exercise on hard surfaces; (d) blows or other injuries; (e) the pull exerted on the bone and its covering by the extensor and flexor muscles of the carpus (the oblique extensor and the flexor carpi radialis muscles have tendons inserted on the head of the inner small metacarpal bone).

Inflammation of the periosteum covering the metacarpal bones may give rise to the condition, which is common in racehorses, known as sore shins. This results from concussion but may also be influenced by the pull of tendons, notably that of the extensor carpi radialis. It is a condition which is more common in young, immature bone, though some animals may be prone to it throughout life.

The Small Metacarpal Bones

The small metacarpals represent abortive long bones lacking any medullary cavity. The inner bone is usually larger than the outer, but each is three-sided and slightly curved with the concavity directed

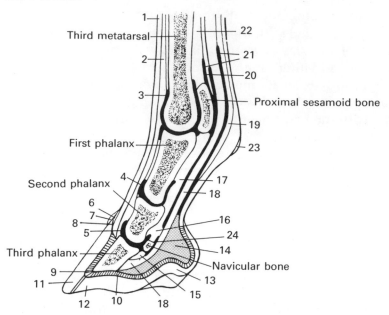

Fig. 29 Diagrammatic section of the limb below the knee.
(1) Skin.   (2) Common digital extensor tendon.   (3) Capsule of fetlock joint.
(4) Capsule of pastern joint.   (5) Capsule of coffin joint.   (6) Corium of
periople.   (7) Periople.   (8) Coronary corium.   (9) Laminar corium.
(10) Corium of sole.   (11) Wall.   (12) Sole.   (13) Frog.   (14) Digital cushion.
(15) Distal ligament of navicular.   (16) Suspensory ligament of navicular.
(17) Inferior sesamoidean ligament.   (18) Deep flexor tendon.   (19) Superficial
flexor tendon.   (20) Ring formed from superficial flexor tendon.   (21) Digital
synovial sheath.   (22) Suspensory ligament.   (23) Ergot.   (24) Navicular bursa.

outwards. The upper ends aid in the support of the lower row of carpal
bones. The inner articulates with the second and third carpal bones,
the outer with the fourth. The lower end of each terminates in a small
rounded button.

The Phalanges

The First Phalanx

This is a long bone − defined as such because it has a medullary cavity
− occupying an oblique position between the lower end of the large
metacarpal and the upper end of the *second phalanx* (Fig. 29). Its upper

extremity is deeply grooved and divided into two articular surfaces moulded upon the lower end of the large metacarpal bone. The inner section is usually larger and wider, as a result of which the foot travels forward in a straight line with the midplane of the body and without unnecessary deviation in either lateral or medial directions. However, slight abnormalities or deviations in the relative sizes of the divided segments may be hereditary and accordingly transmitted to progeny. This may give rise to impairment of gait with faulty action of the lower part of the limb.

The lower end of the first phalanx is also divided into two articular surfaces with the inner surface larger, but the line of division is not as distinct as at the upper end. At the front of the upper end there is a prominence for an attachment of the common digital extensor tendon, while at the back of the lower end on either side the superficial flexor tendon attaches.

The Second Phalanx

This is a short bone without a medullary cavity and is therefore solid throughout. It is important because it is partly inside and partly above the upper limit of the wall of the hoof (Fig. 29), and also because of being the first free limb bone to sustain concussion as the foot hits the ground. This is possibly why it is involved in the condition known as ringbone, where it projects above the hoof to support the coronet. True low ringbone — situated on the coronet — is not so common today, due to the virtual disappearance of working horses. The condition in Thoroughbreds occurs most frequently now as a result of direct trauma.

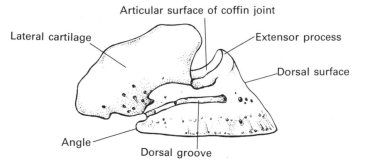

Fig. 30 Third phalanx in lateral view.

The bone is easily felt as it projects above the hoof. Some cases of low ringbone commence at the extensor process (*pyramidal process*) on the front of the upper end of the *third phalanx*, and extend to the second phalanx later. This condition may have an hereditary element to it.

The second phalanx lies somewhat obliquely and is supported along its posterior surface by the deep flexor tendon which runs along a groove which is covered by a plate of fibrocartilage. As with the first phalanx, the common extensor tendon has an attachment to the front surface of the second phalanx, and the superficial flexor tendon has an attachment to the back surface. The fact that this bone is not upright, and that it is supported by the deep flexor tendon, probably does a great deal to lesson the degree of concussion it is obliged to withstand.

The Third Phalanx

This terminal bone of the limb much resembles the hoof in shape (Fig. 30), but is very much smaller and occupies only a minor portion of the cavity within the hoof. The wall, or front, surface of the bone slopes downward and forward and is roughened and pitted by numerous holes. The volar, or under, surface is divided by a curved line, the *semilunar crest*, into a crescent-shaped sole in front, and a flexor surface behind. The deep flexor tendon is attached by a fan-like tendon to the edges of the semilunar crest and the flexor surface (Fig. 28B). A space is left between the deep flexor and upper part of the hind face of the bone which is occupied by the distal sesamoid (navicular) bone (Fig. 28). Beneath the third phalanx and the deep flexor tendon there is a space filled by a fibroelastic pad known as the *digital cushion* (Fig. 29). This pad is moulded over the inner face of the *horny frog* into which it is partly embedded by *papillae* which enter pores in the horn structure. The purpose of the digital cushion is to act as a buffer and lessen concussion when the foot meets the ground.

The third phalanx is well supported within the horny wall of the hoof owing to the presence of *sensitive laminae*, coming from the *corium* covering the bone, which interleave with *horny, insensitive laminae* lining the wall. Its surface is punctuated by small holes through which blood vessels pass into and out of the bone. The vascular system within the hoof is complicated but basically consists of two *terminal digital*

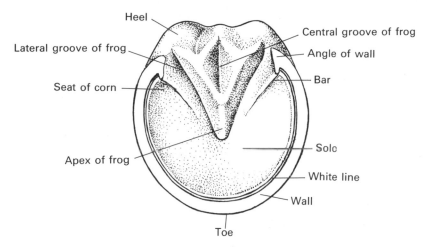

Fig. 31 Undersurface of the right forefoot.

arteries which enter the third phalanx one on either side of its under-surface (Fig. 28). These arteries meet and coalesce in the centre of the bone. The *terminal arch* so produced gives off a large number of radiating branches which pass through bony canals and emerge dorsally to supply all the tissues inside the hoof. Blood flow is directed away from the foot through a complex interwoven network of veins, the *coronary plexus*, encircling the third phalanx, and covering the terminal part of the extensor tendon and the cartilages of the third phalanx.

The highest point of the third phalanx is the *extensor process* at the front of the articular surface. This gives attachment to the tendon of the common digital extensor which advances the foot and extends the fetlock and knee joints. The articular surface is moulded to that of the lower end of the second phalanx. It also carries a flattened facet at its most posterior portion which articulates with the distal sesamoid bone.

The *angles* of the third phalanx on either side are divided into two processes by a deep notch which in aged horses becomes converted into a *foramen* by bone deposition. The two angles give support to the cartilages of the foot (Fig. 30). These are composed of *hyaline cartilage* in the young animal but later become fibrous. Their outer surface is convex and inner concave. On the inner aspect they join up with the digital cushion, and, in front, afford protection to the articulation be-tween the second and third phalanges (the coffin joint). The upper

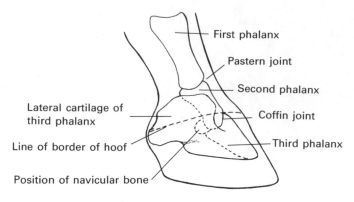

First phalanx

Pastern joint

Second phalanx

Lateral cartilage of
third phalanx

Coffin joint

Line of border of hoof

Third phalanx

Position of navicular bone

Fig. 32 Diagram to show the position of the lateral cartilage in relation to the surface of the foot.

border of each cartilage is thin and flexible and can be moved sideways with the fingers. It bulges outwards every time weight falls on the heel and frog.

In older horses the cartilages often become infiltrated with bone and then the angles of the third phalanx are larger than normal. The cartilages are normally felt at the hinder and lateral edges of the coronet above the heel and quarter when the foot is lifted off the ground. It is easy to determine whether they are free and supple or if they have become calcified. The process of calcification commences at the front and is referred to as sidebone. Lameness may result, but the majority of horses exhibiting calcified cartilages go sound unless there is some other lesion present as well.

Considering all factors, we can see how the foot succeeds in maintaining an efficient circulation. Blood reaches it under the combined influence of gravity and the pumping action of the heart; but the return is helped a great deal by the way the frog is compressed when the foot lands on the ground. This causes the elastic digital cushion to be thrust upwards between the cartilages exerting pressures sufficient to squeeze blood out of the vessels and back up the veins to the body. It must be stressed that this can only be effected when the frog actually makes contact with the ground. If the frog has been trimmed well back and the heel of the shoe is thick, the pumping action may be reduced. Congestion may result and there is a tendency to contraction.

In front, the sole of the hoof presents a rounded or convex border by which it is intimately connected with the lower border of the wall. In the clean, unshod foot this line of union is quite visible just inside the inner margin of the wall and is known as the white line (Fig. 31). At the hinder part of the sole it can be seen to turn inwards and forwards to form an inner lining to the bars. When nailing on a shoe it is important that the nail neither punctures this division between horny and sensitive parts, nor presses unduly on it to cause nail-binding.

The Sesamoid Bones

Proximal Sesamoids

These two small bones lie one on either side at the back of the fetlock, behind the lower end of the large metacarpal bone, with which they articulate. Each sesamoid is a three-sided pyramid. The anterior face is concave and moulded to correspond with the hinder end of the metacarpal bone at its lower end. The posterior surface of each bone lies beside its fellow to provide a smooth channel which is further covered by fibro-cartilage, the *intersesamoidean ligament*. At this level the superficial flexor tendon is in the form of a ring through which the deep flexor tendon glides (Fig. 29). These tendons are bound down in the sesamoid groove by the *volar annular ligament* of the fetlock joint.

The sesamoids act together to form a pulley over which the deep flexor tendon runs. The tendons are thus moved away from the centre of rotation (the joint axis) imparting a considerable increase in leverage. This mechanical advantage is utilised in resisting rotation of the *metacarpo-phalangeal joint* (fetlock). The sesamoids are also bound into the suspensory apparatus by very strong ligaments above, below, laterally and transversely. The suspensory apparatus serves to increase the surface area of the fetlock joint and to receive the compression force transmitted down from the large metacarpal bone above. It can be well understood that these two bones are subjected to a very great degree of strain and overwhelming pressure on occasion. However it is also clear that nature has provided them with a very strong system of bonding to protect them from the normal forces involved.

Distal Sesamoid

The distal sesamoid or navicular bone is small and shuttle shaped, lying behind the articulation between second and third phalanges. Its articular surface is directed upwards and forwards to meet the hinder part of the lower articular surface of the second phalanx. Its lower edge has another articular portion anteriorly in the form of a transversely elongated, flat facet which articulates with a similar surface at the back of the third phalanx between its two heel-like projections.

The tendon surface of the navicular bone is directed downwards and backwards. It is covered by fibrocartilage to make a smooth bed over which the deep flexor tendon travels before it spreads out in fan-like fashion to insert into the semilunar crest on the undersurface of the third phalanx (Figs. 28B and 29).

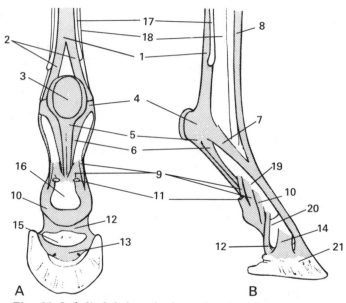

Fig. 33 Left limb below the knee showing the suspensory apparatus.
A. Posterior view. B. Lateral view.
(1) Suspensory ligament.   (2) Bifurcation of ligament.   (3) Intersesamoidean ligament.   (4) Collateral sesamoidean ligament.   (5) Straight distal sesamoidean ligament.   (6) Oblique distal sesamoidean ligament.   (7) Suspensory ligament branch to common extensor tendon.   (8) Common extensor tendon.
(9) Volar ligaments of pastern joint.   (10) Lateral ligaments of pastern joint.
(11) Cut stump of superficial flexor tendon.   (12) Suspensory ligament of navicular.   (13) Distal navicular ligament.   (14) Collateral ligament of coffin joint.
(15) Navicular bone.   (16) Fibrous plate.   (17) Small metacarpal.   (18) Large metacarpal.   (19) First phalanx.   (20) Second phalanx.   (21) Third phalanx.

The Suspensory Apparatus

A number of important ligaments are connected with the sesamoid bones to form the suspensory apparatus, an integral part of the overall *stay apparatus* to be outlined later. The sesamoid bones are an intimate part of this, as are the ligaments. The arrangement of the suspensory apparatus will be better understood by reference to Fig. 33.

The *suspensory* or *superior sesamoidean ligament* lies in the metacarpal groove originating from the back of the lower row of carpal bones and the adjacent part of the large metacarpal bone. It divides into two branches lower down, one passing to each of the proximal sesamoid bones. The ligament then passes forward to the front surface of the first phalanx to join the tendon of the common digital extensor on either side.

The *intersesamoidean ligament* has already been mentioned as the mass of fibrocartilage in which the proximal sesamoid bones are largely embedded, the underside forming a smooth groove for the deep flexor tendon.

The *collateral sesamoidean ligaments* lie on either side of the fetlock joint extending from the proximal sesamoid bones to the lower end of the large metacarpal bone and to the upper end of the first phalanx.

The *inferior sesamoidean ligaments* are a series of separate ligaments running down from the sesamoid bones onto the first phalanx (and also in one case the second phalanx). These are all digital continuations of the suspensory ligament.

The suspensory ligament, being a modified muscle, still contains some muscle tissue and possesses considerable elasticity. Its principal function is to support the fetlock joint, preventing excessive dorsiflexion (overextension). As we shall see later, this supporting function is aided by the tendons of both superficial and deep flexor muscles. The suspensory ligament together with the proximal sesamoid bones carries most of the weight of the horse at many stages of locomotion.

The Fetlock Joint

The fetlock joint is another typical ginglymus, exhibiting only flexion and extension movements. It is however subjected to the greatest stress of any limb joint, because at times the entire body weight may bear down on a single fetlock. In the normal standing position the joint capsule is extensive behind and allows for a great deal of movement. Overextension is limited by the sesamoidean apparatus, together with the fetlocks own collateral ligaments. Volar flexion is limited only by contact of the heel with the metacarpus.

The Pastern Joint

The pastern joint (*proximal interphalangeal joint*) lies between the first and second phalanges and is the least movable of the phalangeal joints; in the normal standing position it is extended. A small amount of volar flexion is possible but is limited by the tendon of the common digital extensor in front, and possibly, at some stages of movement, by the suspensory ligament extensions from the sesamoids onto the common extensor tendon behind. Excessive dorsiflexion is prevented by the *collateral ligaments* of the joint and by *volar ligaments* on the underside between the first and second phalanges. These volar ligaments thus have considerable importance in bearing weight at the back of the digit. The *straight ligament* (one of the inferior sesamoidean group) attaches onto the second phalanx and helps to support the pastern joint.

The Coffin Joint

The coffin joint (*distal interphalangeal joint*) lies within the hoof between the second and third phalanges. It exhibits a great degree of movement and so has a structure which approaches that of the fetlock rather than the pastern joint. On the underside the navicular bone takes part in the formation of the joint, and has a series of specific ligaments associated with it. These are somewhat elastic and form a suspensory apparatus involved in digital support. These *suspensory navicular ligaments* are attached at their upper ends to the lower part of the second phalanx blending with the pastern ligaments as they pass down to attach to the navicular bone. The navicular bone is supported below by the *distal navicular ligament* passing onto the semilunar crest area of the third phalanx. In the normal standing position the joint is extended, overextension being limited by the suspensory apparatus and the deep flexor tendon behind.

5 The Hind Limb

The hind limb differs from the fore in the fact that it is directly attached, through bony union, with the spine. This means that propulsive forces generated by the hind limbs will be transmitted directly onto the vertebral column, but it also means that concussive forces are transmitted to it through the limb.

From above to below the bones of the hind limb are:

  a. The *os coxae* or pelvic bone.
  b. The *femur*, which reaches from the hip joint to the stifle (the large sesamoid bone, the *patella*, lies at the front of the lower end of the femur).
  c. The *tibia* and *fibula*, extending from the stifle to the hock joint (the fibula is greatly reduced in extent).
  d. The *tarsus* or hock, made up of six bones.
  e. The *metatarsal bones* and *phalanges*, which differ in no significant respects from the metacarpals and phalanges of the forelimb.

The Pelvic Girdle

The pelvic girdle consists of two equal halves made up of bones which are welded together in adult life (Fig. 35). These bones, together with the sacrum and the first three coccygeal vertebrae, form the bony walls of the pelvis surrounding the pelvic cavity. This cavity houses the rectum and bladder (when empty), the posterior part of the uterus, vagina and vulva in the mare, and some parts of the genital tract of the stallion. In the mare it also provides the passage through which the foetus must pass during the process of birth.

Each half of the girdle is made up of three flat bones — the *ilium*, the *ischium* and the *pubis* — fused together into one composite bone.

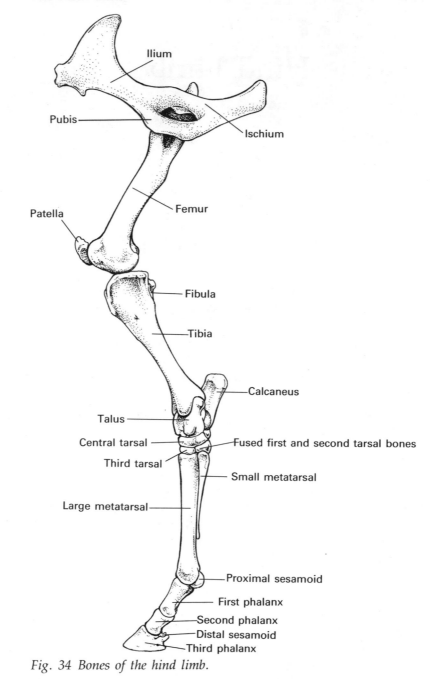

Fig. 34 Bones of the hind limb.

The upper portion of the pelvic bone − that part which attaches to the sacrum − is the ilium; the front of the pelvic floor lying between the hind limbs consists of the pubis, and the hindmost portion is formed by the ischium. These three bones all meet at one point and in so doing give rise to the large, cup-shaped, articular cavity known as the *acetabulum*, which houses the head of the femur to form the hip joint.

The ilium is the largest of the pelvic bones. It is flattened above into a roughly triangular plate which forms part of the roof and outer wall of the pelvic cavity. Its outermost angle is enlarged to form the *tuber coxae* which gives shape to the *haunch* or *pin*, the most prominent bony part of the hindquarters on either side. The inner angle of the triangular, upper part of the ilium, the *tuber sacrale*, approximates its fellow of the other side where they join the sacrum, being firmly united to it by the short, strong *sacroiliac ligament*. At the highest point of the hindquarters the two sides of the tuber sacrale together form the slight eminence known as the croup.

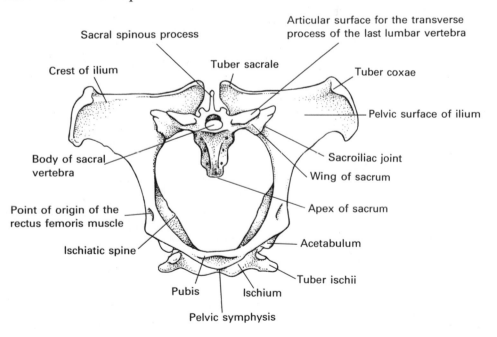

Fig. 35 Pelvis in anteroventral view showing the relationship of the pelvic bones and sacrum.

The pubis and ischium combine to form the pelvic floor and meet their opposite numbers at the *pelvic symphysis* mid-ventrally. In the foal the bones are joined by a layer of fibrocartilage. In the adult this is largely replaced by bone and no appreciable movement occurs even in the mare. The *obturator foramen* is a large perforation on either side of the pelvic symphysis between the pubis and ischium; it is covered by a membranous sheet for the most part but gives passage to nerves and blood vessels. The ischium is thickened at the back as the *tuber ischii* or *seat bone*.

The Pelvic Cavity

The pelvic cavity is the last of the three major body cavities, the others being the thorax and abdomen. It is tubular in shape and continuous with the abdominal cavity, though the pubic bones cross the front end of the pelvic floor transversely and limit entry to the pelvis from the abdomen. The size of the pelvis is really only of concern when a mare is foaling, and then it is only in relation to the size of the foal about to pass through it. Fortunately, relative oversize of the foetus is not a major problem encountered in foaling, as it is in cattle for example.

The boundaries of the pelvic cavity become apparent when internal examination is made per rectum. The roof is formed by the sacrum, the first three coccygeal vertebrae and the flattened, triangular portions of the ilia. The walls are supported by the two shafts of the ilia, one on either side, and also by a tense membranous sheet consisting of the *lateral sacroiliac* and *sacrosciatic ligaments* (Fig. 36). This composite sheet fills the space between the sacrum and first pair of coccygeal bones and the ilium and ischium. The lower border of the ligament leaves two gaps between it and the border of the pelvic bone, these are the *greater* and *lesser sciatic foramina* for the passage of nerves and blood vessels to the muscles of the rump and much of the hind leg. The hind border of the ligament is fused with part of the *semimembranosus* muscle which originates from the first two coccygeal vertebrae and from the sacrosciatic ligament itself. The floor of the pelvic cavity is made up of the pubic bones and ischia on either side of the pelvic symphysis.

The pelvic bones provide extensive areas for muscle attachment, many of which are especially important in locomotion. The tuber coxae and the adjacent part of the ilium give origin to the *tensor fasciae latae*

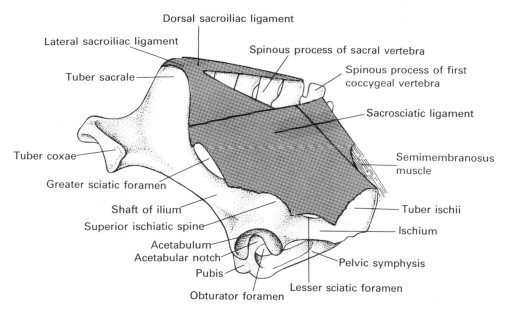

Dorsal sacroiliac ligament

Lateral sacroiliac ligament

Spinous process of sacral vertebra

Tuber sacrale

Spinous process of first coccygeal vertebra

Sacrosciatic ligament

Tuber coxae

Semimembranosus muscle

Greater sciatic foramen

Shaft of ilium

Superior ischiatic spine

Tuber ischii

Acetabulum

Ischium

Acetabular notch

Pubis

Pelvic symphysis

Obturator foramen

Lesser sciatic foramen

Fig. 36 Pelvis in lateral view showing the ligamentous wall of the pelvic cavity.

and the *superficial gluteal* muscles. The remainder of the iliac shaft and the outer face of the sacrosciatic ligament give origin to the middle and deep gluteal muscles. Behind the hip joint the sacrosciatic ligament, the first two coccygeal vertebrae, and the tuber ischii give origin to the hamstring muscles (*biceps femoris, semitendinosus* and *semimembranosus*). On the inner side of the hip the ventral parts of the ischium and pubis, in the region of the pelvic symphysis, give origin to the *gracilis* and *adductor* muscles.

The front opening of the pelvic cavity, the *pelvic inlet*, faces obliquely downwards and forwards. The size and shape of this differs between the sexes. The external diameter of the pelvis determines the width of the horse's hindquarters, while the internal diameter varies, being wider and more circular in the mare, narrower and more upright in the stallion and gelding.

The cavity of the female pelvis is considerably larger than that of the male, the acetabula are farther apart and so are the seat bones, thus the *pelvic outlet* is larger. The obturator foramina are also larger in the mare and the pelvic floor is wider and flatter. The overall diameter of the inside of the pelvis is also influenced by the angle at which the sacrum lies in relation to the pelvic floor. When the sacrum is tilted downwards it may partially occlude the pelvic entrance or at least make it smaller. This may cause difficulty in foaling. Difficulty may also arise when the sacrum is excessively long, but horizontal, and when the distance between the seat bones and the haunches is great.

The Hip Joint

This joint (Fig. 37) is made up from the head of the femur and the acetabulum. The latter is a deep articular cup situated at the junction of the ilium, pubis and ischium. The rim of this *cotyloid cavity* is deeply cut into medially by the *acetabular notch*. The total depth of the cup is increased by the presence of an added fibrocartilaginous ring, the *cotyloid ligament*, attached to the bony rim of the acetabulum. Part of the cotyloid ligament crosses the acetabular notch as the *transverse acetabular ligament*. The whole of the surface of the bowl is not covered with articular cartilage and a corresponding *non-articular notch* is present on the head of the femur. Into these gaps two structures are attached.

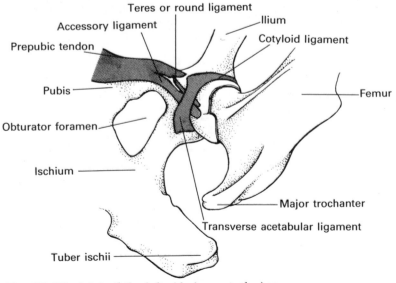

Fig. 37 Hip joint of the left side in ventral view.

One is the short round or *teres ligament* passing from the head of the femur into the articular gap in the acetabular bowl, the other is the *accessory ligament*; a structure present only in the horse family. This originates from the opposite *prepubic tendon* of the abdominal muscles. It crosses its fellow tendon in front of the pubis and enters the acetabulum through the acetabular notch, held in place by the transverse acetabular ligament. Inside the acetabulum it is attached to the non-articular surface of the femoral head alongside the teres ligament.

The prominence on the outer side of the thigh usually referred to as the hip joint is, in reality, the *major trochanter* of the femur. The true hip joint lies several inches deeper and cannot be felt from the exterior.

The joint capsule is a double-mouthed sac attached around the head of the femur at one end and around the rim of the acetabulum at the other. The joint permits movement in every direction although the accessory ligament limits ability to abduct the hind limb (move it away from the body). This is said to make it difficult for a horse to cow-kick in the forward and outward direction — but do not depend on it! The mule and donkey both manage to execute this manoeuvre with ease.

Most textbooks infer that the hip joint of the horse has a greater range of movement than any other joint in the body. This should be taken to refer to direction rather than extent. The accessory ligament is tensed so promptly by any inward rotation of the thigh that this movement is almost non-existent. In a horse standing squarely on all four feet the ileo-femoral angle (the angle in front of the hip joint) is 110–115 degrees; the inclination of the femur to the vertical is 80 degrees and that of the ilium 30–35 degrees with the horizontal. When the hip is flexed the femur travels forwards but in actual practice its range of movement is limited by the fact that the thigh is closely attached to the body. This is unlike the dog in which the thigh is long and the femur free throughout the greater part of its length. Not only has the dog this freely operating femur, but its extremely flexible back actually bends downwards during the act of galloping until the loin becomes, as it were, continuous with the thigh, thus increasing the length of the stride. As already said, the horse, in contrast, is inhibited here and its hind feet seldom advance forward even in a fast gallop beyond a line dropped from the umbilicus. Those of a greyhound shoot past the forelimbs, and the hind feet, at faster gaits, may land on the ground at the level of the point of the shoulder (Fig. 1).

The Femur

This is a long bone, one of the heaviest and strongest in the body yet like the humerus it can be shattered in the middle of a flat race by muscular incoordination. The femur acts as the medium between two very important joints, hip and stifle, and is specially adapted for providing attachment for the large muscles which operate the upper part of the limb (Fig. 38).

It carries at its upper end a hemispherical articular head which fits accurately into the cavity of the acetabulum and has a non-articular pit which gives attachment to the *round* and *accessory ligaments*. These ligaments serve to hold the head of the femur and acetabulum in close approximation. On the outer side of the upper end of the bone is the *major trochanter*. From this eminence a strong ridge descends to merge with another large prominence almost halfway down the shaft of the bone — the *third trochanter*. These two trochanters serve for the insertion of the three major parts of the gluteal muscles; the deep and middle gluteals insert onto the major trochanter, the superficial gluteal onto the third trochanter. On the inner surface of the shaft at the level of the third trochanter is the *minor trochanter* to which the *iliopsoas* muscle is attached.

Much of the shaft of the femur is given over to muscle attachment. Its front surface, and a great deal of both inner and outer surfaces, give origin to the three heads of the *vastus* muscles which comprise the bulk of the *quadriceps femoris* muscle group. Its posterior surface has part of the *biceps femoris* muscle inserting near the third trochanter and practically all the *adductor* muscle from the third trochanter down.

In front, the lower end of the femur carries a double, nearly vertical, pulley-like groove known as the *trochlea*. The *inner trochlear lip* is much fuller and extends up higher than the outer, and the two converge below. Thus the trochlea provides a smooth, V-shaped groove, well reinforced with fibrocartilage to increase the depth, in which the patella glides up and down. On the reverse side of the lower end of the femur are the *medial* and *lateral condyles* separated by the *intercondyloid fossa*. These form the upper section of the true stifle joint articulating with the head of the tibia and with the intra-articular fibrocartilages. Between the lateral condyle and the trochlea is the *extensor fossa*, a depression in which the common tendon of origin of the long *digital extensor* and the

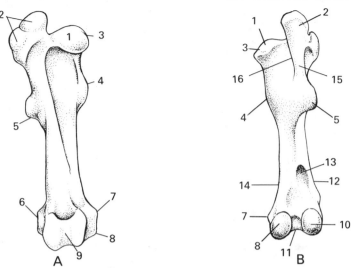

Fig. 38 Femur of the right side. A. Anterior view. B. Posterior view.
(1) Head.   (2) Major trochanter.   (3) Fovea.   (4) Minor trochanter.   (5) Third
trochanter.   (6) Lateral epicondyle.   (7) Medial epicondyle.   (8) Medial
condyle.   (9) Trochlea.   (10) Lateral condyle.   (11) Intercondyloid fossa.
(12) Lateral supracondyloid crest.   (13) Supracondyloid fossa.   (14) Medial
supracondyloid crest.   (15) Trochanteric ridge.   (16) Trochanteric fossa.

peroneus tertius muscles are attached. Above the condyles on the hind
surface are both *medial* and *lateral supracondyloid ridges* giving origin
to the two heads of the *gastrocnemius muscle*. These ridges flank the
supracondyloid fossa and are the origin of the *superficial flexor* muscle.
Medial and *lateral epicondyles* are present between the condyles and the
ridges of the trochlea. The medial epicondyle is the more pronounced
and gives insertion to parts of both the semimembranosus and adductor
muscles.

The Tibia and Fibula

The tibia is a long bone extending obliquely down and back
between the stifle and hock joints (Fig. 39). The upper end is divided
into a *tibial tuberosity*, a non-articular prominence for attachment of the
patellar ligaments, while behind it on each side of the tibial head is an
articular surface composed of medial and lateral condyles. The condyles
are slightly concave and separated by a sharp raised prominence, the

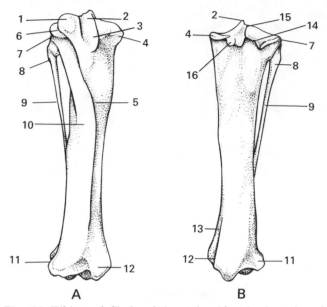

Fig. 39 Tibia and fibula of the right side. A. Anterior view. B. Posterior view.

(1) Tibial tuberosity.   (2) Tibial spine.   (3) Groove for middle patellar ligament.
(4) Medial condyle.   (5) Tibial crest.   (6) Muscular groove.   (7) Lateral condyle.
(8) Head of fibula.   (9) Shaft of fibula.   (10) Shaft of tibia.   (11) Lateral
malleolus.   (12) Medial malleolus.   (13) Groove for long digital extensor.
(14) Popliteal notch.   (15) Fossa for anterior cruciate ligament.   (16) Tubercle
for posterior cruciate ligament.

tibial spine. The upper end of the *tibial shaft* provides attachment areas for muscles acting on the hock and digits. The most important is the deep digital flexor coming from the region of the lateral condyle and the posterior surface of the shaft of the tibia (and fibula). The lateral digital extensor and anterior tibial muscles also arise from the region of the lateral condyle and the lateral surface of the shaft.

The lower end of the tibia carries an articular surface composed of two deep articular grooves separated by an articular ridge. This whole surface is moulded upon the similar ridges and grooves in the talus, the bone of the hock with which it articulates. These ridges and grooves in both bones are set obliquely forwards and outwards. It is extremely important that this particular angle of obliquity be exactly correct; the whole movement of the lower portion of the limb being linked with it.

The fibula is a much reduced long bone articulating with the outer surface of the lateral tibial condyle. It is a thin bone, not unlike a small metacarpal (splint) bone, which tapers away to a point at the lower third of the tibial shaft. Between the bodies of the tibia and fibula is an elongated *interosseus space*. The lower end of the fibula is fused with the tibia, forming the *lateral malleolus*.

The Stifle Joint

Just as the carpus of the horse is analogous with the human wrist, so the stifle corresponds with the human knee and the hock with the human ankle. The stifle contains two separate articulations; one between the tibia and femur, the *femorotibial articulation*; the other between the patella and femur, the *femoropatellar articulation*.

The Femorotibial Articulation

This joint (Figs. 40 and 41) consists of the condyles of the femur articulating with the condylar surfaces of the tibial head. These articular surfaces are not adapted to one another except by a small area of contact centrally; interposed between them are two plates of fibrocartilage, the *menisci* or intra-articular cartilages. The outer edges of these crescentic cartilages are thick and convex, while the inner are concave, thin and translucent. The lower surface of each is flat and rests on the condylar surface of the tibia. The upper surface is concave to receive the femoral condyle.

The menisci are held in place by fibrous *meniscal ligaments*, attached to the head in front and behind the tibial spine. The lateral meniscus also has an additional attachment posteriorly to the intercondyloid fossa of the femur (Fig. 40B). The ligaments of the joint itself, a ginglymus joint, are in the form of normal medial and lateral collateral ligaments. In addition, two strong fibrous cords, the *cruciate ligaments*, are situated mainly in the intercondyloid fossa, crossing each other like the letter X, and attaching tibia to femur. These ligaments do not lie in a saggital plane but are twisted slightly so that outward rotation of the leg untwists and slackens them.

The menisci function to correct the disparity between the femoral condyles and the articular surfaces of the tibia, and they act also as

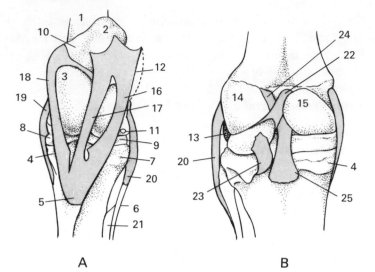

Fig. 40 Stifle joint of the left side. A. Anterior view. B. Posterior view.
(1) Femur. (2) Patella. (3) Medial ridge of trochlea. (4) Medial condyle of
tibia. (5) Tibial tuberosity. (6) Fibula. (7) Lateral condyle of tibia.
(8) Medial meniscus. (9) Lateral meniscus. (10) Accessory cartilage of
patella. (11) Stump of extensor longus and peroneus tertius. (12) Insertion of
biceps femoris muscle. (13) Stump of popliteus tendon. (14) Lateral condyle
of femur. (15) Medial condyle of femur. (16) Lateral patellar ligament.
(17) Middle patellar ligament. (18) Medial patellar ligament. (19) Medial
femorotibial ligament. (20) Lateral femorotibial ligament. (21) Interosseous
ligament. (22) Femoral ligament of lateral meniscus. (23) Posterior ligament
of lateral meniscus. (24) Anterior cruciate ligament. (25) Posterior cruciate
ligament.

shock absorbers. The cruciate ligaments and the collateral ligaments
function to prevent overextension.

The Femoropatellar Articulation

This joint occurs between the trochlea of the femur and the patella. The
patella is a sesamoid bone and performs essentially the same functions
as the proximal sesamoids of the fetlock. It provides a mechanical
advantage for the quadriceps muscle of the thigh, a stifle extensor, by
removing its line of action further from the centre of rotation of the
joint. The patella, although not weight bearing, also provides a compression and tension resistant element for the quadriceps femoris

tendon. It transmits the muscular pull exerted upon it to the tibia through three long ligamentous cords, the *patellar ligaments* (Fig. 40A). These ligaments are inserted into the tuberosity of the head of the tibia and are palpable in the living animal immediately below the patella. The middle patellar ligament which is the strongest has a special groove on the tibial tuberosity scooped out for its reception (Fig. 39B). These ligaments are actually tendons of insertion of the quadriceps muscle mass of the thigh. The lateral patellar ligament also receives a strong tendon from the biceps femoris and the tensor fasciae latae muscles through the attachment to it of the fascia lata of the thigh. The middle patellar ligament is only concerned with the *vastus* and the *rectus femoris* muscle insertions. The medial patellar ligament is the weakest of the three and is joined also by a diffuse tendon from the *gracilis* and *sartorius* muscles of the inner side of the thigh.

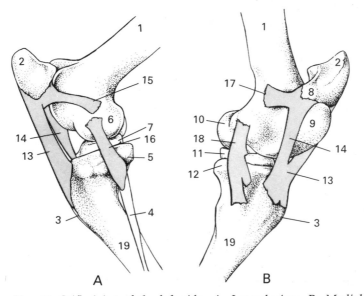

Fig. 41 Stifle joint of the left side. A. Lateral view. B. Medial view.
(1) Femur. (2) Patella. (3) Tibial tuberosity. (4) Fibula. (5) Lateral condyle of tibia. (6) Lateral condyle of femur. (7) Lateral meniscus. (8) Accessory fibro-cartilage of the patella. (9) Medial ridge of trochlea. (10) Medial condyle of femur. (11) Medial meniscus. (12) Medial condyle of tibia. (13) Middle patellar ligament. (14) Medial patellar ligament. (15) Lateral femoropatellar ligament. (16) Lateral femorotibial ligament. (17) Medial femoropatellar ligament. (18) Medial femorotibial ligament. (19) Tibia

The patella carries on its inner, articular surface a central vertical ridge separating two small concave areas on either side. The ridge fits into the groove on the femoral trochlea, but the lateral areas on the patella do not fit the ridges of the trochlea at all accurately. The inner, concave patellar area, like the inner trochlear ridge, is much the wider of the two and these surfaces are brought together by the curved accessory fibrocartilage.

Movement of the Stifle Joint

The stifle is another ginglymus joint with principal movements of flexion and extension. In the normal standing position the angle behind the stifle varies from 135 to 140 degrees. Flexion of the joint is limited only by contact of the leg with the thigh. Extension, however, is incomplete as the thigh and leg bones never come into the same straight line, further movement being checked by the tension of the collateral and cruciate ligaments.

During stifle flexion and extension there may be times when the patella is in danger of slipping out of its trochlear groove, but the risk of dislocation is reduced somewhat by the medial and lateral femoro-patellar ligaments. Thus it is unusual for the patella to be pulled over the rim of the trochlea either internally or externally during motion. More commonly it is pulled in an upward direction where it can hook itself over the upper end of the inner trochlear ridge while the horse is at rest (Fig. 41B). This patellar or stifle locking mechanism, which is of great importance in the resting position, occurs when the joint is subjected to a degree of extension not occurring during normal loco-motion. In the resting position, however, flexion of the stifle is pre-vented as long as the hip is flexed, since in hip flexion outward rotation of the femur occurs seating the medial patellar ligament firmly on the medial trochlear ridge. In this state stifle flexion jams the patellar ligament system on the medial trochlear ridge and fixes the joint in position.

In order to unlock this system the quadriceps femoris muscle may contract lifting the patella, while the biceps femoris muscle contracts to pull it laterally off the ridge. Also if the hip extends, followed by stifle extension, unlocking should occur.

Abnormal patellar fixation often occurs in horses with straight hind limbs in which inadvertent overextension and subsequent locking are likely to occur in motion, or, more commonly, as the horse prepares to move off. This results in the limb being locked in full extension with the result that, stretched to its utmost, it is carried behind the body. While surgical division of the medial patellar ligament will prevent this, it does not correct the basic cause which is overextension of the stifle joint. Reposition requires veterinary assistance and is usually effected by applying forward traction helped by inducing the horse to make a sudden jump forward on the sound limb. This condition — *patellar luxation in the upward direction* — is frequently encountered in young horses. It may be hereditary and has been associated with certain stallions. In many cases the tendency lessens or disappears when the bones attain full length and growth ceases. Young racing Thoroughbreds suffering from the condition are commonly treated surgically.

The Tarsus or Hock

In the same way as the knee, the hock is made up of several joints (Figs. 42 and 43), however it articulates directly with the lower end of the tibia through only a single bone, the *talus*. The six bones comprising the tarsus are bound together tightly by ligaments. All are short, flat bones and arranged roughly in three rows. In the upper row are the talus and *calcaneus*; in the middle row, the *central tarsal* alone; in the lower row, the *first* and *second tarsals* fused together and the *third tarsal*. The *fourth tarsal*, a six-sided bone shaped like a brick, occupies a part of both middle and lower rows being as deep as the central and third tarsal. It stands alone, directly beneath the calcaneus bone.

The talus is an irregularly shaped bone composed of a pulley-like articular surface or trochlea which conforms with that of the lower end of the tibia. This surface carries two rounded ridges and a deep groove between them. The groove is directed spirally downwards, forwards and outwards, taking nearly a half turn around the bone. The hindside of the bone carries four facets for articulation with the fibular tarsal, together with some roughened surfaces for the attachment of ligaments.

The calcaneus is the largest bone in the hock and is made up of a body with a large upstanding process, the *tuber calcis* (the point of the hock, equivalent to the human heel). Its body is moulded on the

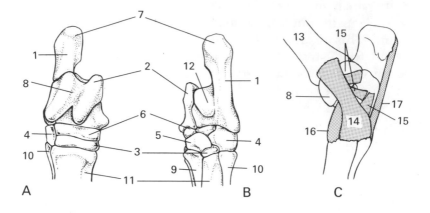

Fig. 42 Tarsus of the right side. A. Anterior view. B. Posterior view.
C. Medial view showing the main ligaments of the hock.
(1) Calcaneus. (2) Talus. (3) Third tarsal. (4) Fourth tarsal. (5) First
tarsal fused with second tarsal. (6) Central tarsal. (7) Tuber calcis.
(8) Trochlea. (9) Second metatarsal. (10) Fourth metatarsal. (11) Large
metatarsal. (12) Tarsal groove for deep flexor tendon. (13) Tibia. (14) Long
medial collateral ligament. (15) Short medial ligaments. (16) Dorsal tarsal
ligaments. (17) Plantar ligament.

posterior surface of the talus and its articular facets, and has on its
lower part a strong, inwardly projecting process, the *sustentaculum tali*.
The lower surface of this projection forms a groove with the main body
of the bone, the *tarsal groove* (Fig. 42B) for the tendon of the deep flexor
muscle. The tuber calcis has an almost flat outer surface; the concave
inner side enters into the formation of the tarsal groove.

The tuber calcis forms a lever arm for the attachment of the extensor
muscles of the hock, especially the gastrocnemius and the tarsal tendon
of the biceps femoris and semitendinosus muscles. The tendon of the
superficial flexor also caps the point of the hock and attaches to its hind
surface. The outer or lateral face is roughened and non-articular and
carries a prominent blunt tuberosity. The inner surface carries a wide,
shallow pit. These both give attachment to the ligaments that bind the
joint together (Figs. 42C and 43B).

The central tarsal is a flattened bone, slightly concave on top for
articulation with the talus. It occupies the whole of the central row,
apart from the fourth tarsal which has the same depth as that of the
central and third tarsals combined.

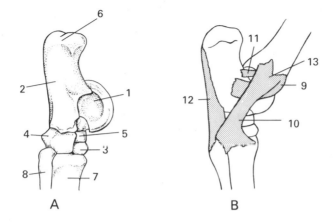

Fig. 43 Tarsus of the right side. A. Lateral view. B. Lateral view showing the main ligaments of the hock.
(1) Talus. (2) Calcaneus. (3) Third tarsal. (4) Fourth tarsal. (5) Central tarsal. (6) Tuber calcis. (7) Large metatarsal. (8) Fourth metatarsal. (9) Short lateral ligaments. (10) Long lateral collateral ligament. (11) Ligament between talus and calcaneus. (12) Plantar ligament. (13) Groove for lateral extens or tendon.

The third tarsal, the flat bone of the lowest row, greatly resembles the central tarsal but is smaller and more triangular in shape. The smallest of all, the fused first and second tarsals, situated on the inner side of the hock, are roughly triangular, with a base at the rear, and apex pointing downwards and forwards.

Various bones of the hock provide attachment for muscles besides those attaching to the tuber calcis. Thus the hock flexors are inserted onto the first tarsal (*anterior tibial* muscle) and third, fourth and calcaneus bones (*peronius tertius* muscle). Both these muscles also attach to the upper end of the large metatarsal bone.

The bones of the hock can be palpated if the skin is not too thick, or the hock too coarse. This exercise is of value in the diagnosis of spavin. True spavin is a bone inflammation which commences on the inner side of the hock near the head of the metatarsal bone and extends into the fused first and second tarsals, and sometimes the central tarsal. It is marked by degeneration of the articular surfaces with deposition of new bony deposits on the external edges; a form of healing process. However, this interferes with the complete flexion of the joint and causes lameness. The lameness is most pronounced when the horse first comes out of its stable but diminishes with exercise; it is most noticeable when the horse is moving off. The condition is said to be hereditary, but it is uncertain whether it is the pathological condition that is transmitted, the conformation, or the quality of bone.

Movement of the Hock Joint

For all practical purposes the hock is a ginglymus joint moving in only one direction, since practically the whole movement takes place between the tibia and talus. In fact more movement takes place between these in the horse than in most other animals and less between the talus and central tarsal. Movement between the remaining bones is very slight. Lateral movement is prevented by the structure of the joint surfaces, although the overall movement is in an oblique direction.

The joint capsule is thin in front but extremely thick on the underside forming the *plantar ligament* (Figs. 42 and 43). This ligament, which is cartilaginous in part, forms a smooth surface for the deep flexor tendon. The capsule also gives rise to the *subtarsal check ligament* which unites lower down with the deep flexor tendon.

In the normal standing position the angle in front of the hock is approximately 150 degrees. Like the elbow and stifle this is the middle position of the joint and the articular surfaces are in maximum contact. Complete extension is prevented by the collateral ligaments; flexion is checked only by contact of the metatarsus with the leg.

The hock joint is one of the hardest working structures in the body, and much of the animal's activity is centred around its ability to flex and extend this joint rapidly and rhythmically with perfect timing. The stifle and hock are synchronised in their movements by virtue of the ligaments and muscles which control them. When the stifle flexes the hock flexes, when the hock extends the stifle extends; one not functioning independently of the other because of the tendinous bands in front of and behind the limb. These are the peroneus tertius and the superficial flexor muscles respectively, extending from the lower part of the femur to the tarsus and metatarsus (Fig. 5).

It follows, therefore, that a horse with a straight stifle carries a straight hock, and vice versa. Thus an animal standing squarely possesses hocks as flexed as its stifles. This would mean that the hocks, if excessively flexed, would be placed far back. A line dropped from the tuber ischii to the ground would not lie, as it should, straight along the posterior edge of the hind limb from hock to fetlock, but down the side or, in an extreme case, even in front of the limb. This implies possession of a particularly long tibia, conformation not regarded by horse breeders with satisfaction because greater speed is derived from a straighter hind limb. The reason for this is that ground is covered faster by a series of rapid short strides rather than by fewer long ones — though rapid longer strides are an evident source of progress in human athletics today.

The bones of the hock, other than the talus, act mainly against concussion. There is very little movement between these, either as rows or individually. The lower end of the tibia fits accurately into its groove, so that in pulley fashion the joint can work smoothly and handle great weights with a minimum degree of muscular effort. Additional leverage provided by the tuber calcis greatly adds to the efficacy of the joint, giving much greater power to the muscles, the tendons of which are attached to its summit.

The remaining portions of the hind limb greatly resemble those of the forelimb. The hind foot is narrower and more upright than the fore, but in each case the outer surface of the sole and wall is a little more convex than the inner which is flatter. The sole of the hind foot is also a little more concave than that of the forefoot.

6   Surface Anatomy

This portion of the book should be read with frequent reference to earlier chapters. The majority of established horsemen and regular riders will be acquainted with most of the surface features depicted in Chart 2. Those who are not should study these preferably by comparing the chart with a living horse. Further study of the bony structures combined with the information given here should provide a more complete picture.

The surface of the body should be studied not only with the eyes but also with the hands. Veterinary surgeons use both, and, when diagnosing bone conditions or the state of tendons and ligaments, firstly employ vision, then confirm findings by examining and comparing suspect and sound parts manually.

The Skin

The skin varies in thickness over various parts of the body and this can be felt with ease, as well as tightness or slackness between it and its attachments beneath. There may be little connective tissue in parts, while at others the fibrous tissue of the *subcutis* may be sponge-like and loose. Wherever danger of injury to the body is great the skin is correspondingly thicker. Hence that covering the back, loins, quarters and limbs is thickest; that covering the face, muzzle, flanks, and inner side of the limbs, may feel almost paper thin to handle. Nevertheless, even the thinnest skin possesses very great tensile strength.

The skin is least thick in the Thoroughbred and Arab, and thickest in the draught breeds. The thickness in ponies varies according to whether they retain their true type or have been crossed with Thoroughbreds. When picked up between finger and thumb the feel of the skin can be misleading, since it may carry a variable amount of subcutaneous fat attached to it. In a horse in good condition, a hand placed flat over the ribs may be moved from side to side, the skin gliding over underlying structures on account of this fat. In a thin horse it will feel firm and immovable as though it were glued to the ribs. Such hidebound animals may be suffering from absence of fat, but may equally be dehydrated and lack fluid in and beneath the skin. This latter problem is a natural result of strong, or prolonged exercise, and is prevented today by the regular administration of electrolytes in water or feed.

The skin consists of two principal layers, the superficial *epidermis* and the deeper *dermis*. Sensory nerve ramifications, blood vessels and glands (both sweat and sebaceous) are present in the dermis. The epidermis is avascular with its outer layer formed of dying and dead cells which eventually are cast off (*desquamate*). The deepest epidermal layer, the *stratum germinativum*, is responsible for regeneration to compensate for this loss. The generative layer also contains *melanin*, a black or brown pigment which absorbs ultraviolet radiation and protects the skin and body from the effects of excessive sunlight.

The epidermis is perforated by the passage of hairs and their follicles and by the ducts of glands. Its principal function is to prevent the penetration of liquids and noxious gases through the skin, and this is aided by fatty secretion from sebaceous glands onto its surface. An important subsidiary function performed by the skin is that of temperature regulation, aided by the hairs and sweat glands. Sensory perception is also one of its attributes and some areas are far more sensitive than others in this regard. Parts such as the lips and muzzle used for making contact with food and nearby objects, are provided with long feeler hairs. These are connected to sensitive roots of associated sensory nerves. Horses use these especially when feeding, both from the ground and from a manger. Mares nuzzle their foals with them and it is possible they recognise their offspring in this way, as well as by sound and the sense of smell.

The Skin Musculature

The skin is attached to the underlying parts by the subcutaneous connective tissue containing elastic fibres and fat, the subcutis. In some parts of the body, notably the neck and back, tenseness is maintained by the presence in the subcutis of a thin voluntary muscle layer, the

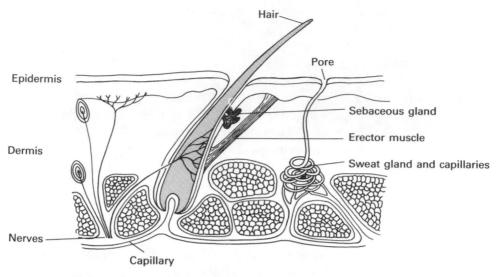

Fig. 44 Section through the skin.

cutaneous muscle, which is adherent to the skin. This muscle has only a limited attachment to the skeleton; the part in the neck attaches to the *cariniform cartilage* at the front of the sternum. The abdominal layer covers a large part of the body behind the shoulder and arm, and has attachments to the medial tuberosity of the humerus in front and the patella above the stifle at the back. On contraction it can twitch the skin and rid the greater part of the body of flies, dust, dirt and other irritants. By being adherent to the skin the cutaneous muscle may create shivering by very rapid contractions; this raises the local temperature by bringing warm blood to the cold surface. In a few places, notably the face, the cutaneous muscle is modified and the skin is less adherent to it.

The Skin Glands

The *sebaceous glands* are minute structures freely distributed throughout the whole of the skin in close association with the hair roots. The *sebum* is not a true secretion but a waxy material which renders the skin pliable and waterproof; it contains substances which are converted into vitamin D by the action of sunlight.

The sebaceous glands are remarkable for the fact that they do not actually secrete sebum but deliver it as a result of the destruction of degenerated and debilitated gland cells. Their nutrition has been cut off by the rapid growth of the outer layers of cells. They squeeze the dying and dead cells towards the centre of the follicle and then into the duct through which the sebum is expelled to the surface. Spread thinly over the individual hairs, sebum is responsible for the gloss of the coat. This spread is helped by regular grooming.

The horse is one of the few hairy animals in which sweating occurs over almost the whole body surface; the exception being the skin of the legs. The frothy sweat that accumulates on the legs after a gallop has trickled down from the belly and the insides of the elbows and thighs. Sweating in animals which possess the necessary apparatus is a continuous process and normally evaporation takes place — except during the fastest gaits — as rapidly as sweat is produced.

It has been estimated that the sweat secretion of a horse grazing out of doors in ordinary summer weather and choosing its own pace averages a fluid loss equivalent to about 6.4 kg (14 lb) of body weight in 24 hours without visible dampening of the body surface. When horses are galloped the resulting loss of fluid is inevitably much greater. Sweating is influenced by external temperature, humidity, length of coat, excitement, environment, work, and pace. A horse may sweat, however, when it is hot or cold. In the latter case sweating arises from nervous stimulation of the adrenal glands causing release of adrenalin into the blood which stimulates particular areas of the brain. It is often this effect, caused by anxiety, which makes a horse sweat prior to a race, even on a cold day. However, it is also a known side effect in animals suffering from some virus infections.

Horses that sweat too freely lose weight, unless the fluid is replaced. This is partly due to loss of blood and tissue fluid — mainly the water content — and this situation tends to be aggravated by the resulting disturbance of electrolytes within the body systems.

Illness can result from oversweating or undersweating. Horses exported from temperate to tropical climates may lose the ability to sweat and may develop a condition known as drycoat. If returned to the cooler climate recovery occurs automatically within a few weeks. It would appear that the sweat glands of these affected horses lose their ability to function. Such animals are useless for racing and if galloped may collapse from heart failure.

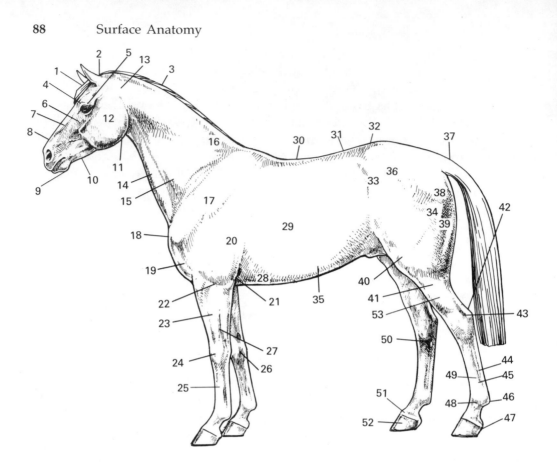

Chart 2 The surface of the horse.
(1) Forelock.   (2) Poll.   (3) Mane.   (4) Forehead.   (5) Temporal muscle in temporal fossa.   (6) Facial crest.   (7) Nasal bone.   (8) Nasal peak. (9) Prominence of chin.   (10) Mandibular ramus.   (11) Larynx. (12) Masseter muscle.   (13) Wing of atlas.   (14) Jugular furrow. (15) Brachiocephalic muscle.   (16) Withers.   (17) Scapular spine.   (18) Point of the shoulder.   (19) Deltoid tuberosity.   (20) Triceps long head.   (21) Point of the elbow.   (22) Site of elbow joint.   (23) Extensor muscles of knee and digit.   (24) Knee.   (25) Metacarpal bones.   (26) Accessory carpal. (27) Flexor muscles of knee and digit.   (28) Pectoral muscles.   (29) Thoracic rib-cage.   (30) Saddle.   (31) Loin.   (32) Croup (tuber sacrale).   (33) Haunch (tuber coxae).   (34) Flank.   (35) Belly.   (36) Quarter.   (37) Tail head or dock.   (38) Seat bone (tuber ischii).   (39) Hamstring muscles. (40) Stifle joint.   (41) Gaskin or second thigh.   (42) Achilles tendon.   (43) Point of hock.   (44) Suspensory ligament.   (45) Flexor tendons.   (46) Ergot. (47) Heel.   (48) Fetlock.   (49) Metatarsal bones.   (50) Chestnut. (51) Coronary band.   (52) Horny wall of foot.   (53) Extensors of digit.

The Hair

Hair covers practically the entire body surface. However, more hair is carried over the parts of the skin exposed to direct sunlight than on the less exposed areas such as the inner surface of the ears, the inner side of the thighs, the perineum and the external genitalia in both sexes.

The skin carries *permanent hair* in the mane and tail, in the feather of some heavy breeds and in the eyelashes and long hairs of the muzzle. Permanent hair goes on growing indefinitely regardless of the temperature changes. The bulk of the hair covering the body is *temporary hair* which is shed and changed for a new growth in spring and autumn, in preparation for the summer and winter coats. This temporary hair consists of closely placed patches of long hairs, 4−5 per sq cm, which tend to hide the undercoat from view. This is made up of densely packed finer and shorter hairs, as many as 650 per sq cm of skin.

Hair plays an important role in temperature regulation. Skin is a poor conductor of heat, especially when left ungroomed and dirty. This is why horses being roughed off are not brushed and encouraged to grow long coats by having their rugs left off. Hair responds in automatic fashion to heat and cold. In a cold atmosphere the hairs tend to rise and form a blanket imprisoning a layer of warm air. In warm weather the coat lies flat, but the skin may be cooled by the evaporation of sweat from its surface. The rise and fall of the hair is due partly to the action of the cutaneous muscle beneath the skin, but mainly to the reflexes of the tiny involuntary muscle fibres attached to each hair follicle in the dermis. In the horse, hair raising is activated by cold but not by fear or anger as in the cat and dog, and occasional human!

The deciding factor in coat casting is temperature, but the number of hours of daylight is also important. If horses are kept under artificial light and heat in winter − as mares frequently are to induce early ovulation − they soon start shedding heavy coats however low the temperature is outside. Similarly, in cold conditions the coat grows rapidly and to a greater length. As a rule the new coat is growing underneath the old and tends to push the latter off. Hard conditions delay coat casting, while good feeding and the provision of oils and essential vitamins will hasten the process. Mares shabby in coat can be slow to conceive and many fail to produce fertile follicles until the new coat has made its appearance. Crossing indigenous ponies with Thoroughbreds or Arabs produces a change in the type of coat. Such animals are less able to withstand winter conditions on moors and hills, or even in open pasture sometimes.

The Head

Now study the external surface of the body referring back for details of bony structures lying beneath each particular feature. First, take a general look over a living horse comparing it with Chart 2 and Fig. 45. After this consider external features in detail and consider the structures which, lying beneath the skin, bring about changes in the contour of the body. A lean animal will be better for this than one so fat you cannot see its ribs.

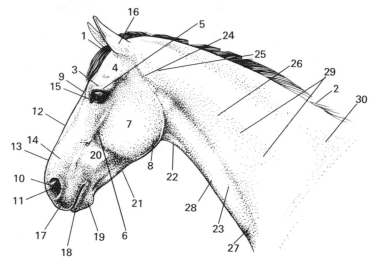

Fig. 45 Landmarks on the surface of the head and neck.
(1) Forelock on forehead. (2) Mane. (3) Supraorbital process of frontal bone. (4) Temporal fossa. (5) Zygomatic arch. (6) Facial crest. (7) Masseter muscle. (8) Angle of mandible. (9) Frontal bone. (10) Outer wing of nostril. (11) Inner wing of nostril. (12) Nasal bone. (13) Nasal peak. (14) Nasomaxillary notch. (15) Nictitating membrane. (16) Conchal cartilage. (17) Upper lip. (18) Lower lip. (19) Prominence of chin. (20) Cheek. (21) Mandibular ramus. (22) Larynx. (23) Jugular furrow. (24) Parotid gland. (25) Wing of atlas. (26) Brachiocephalic muscle. (27) Sternohyoid muscle. (28) Trachea. (29) Transverse processes of cervical vertebrae. (30) Trapezius muscle.

Commencing at the poll note the mane with the forelock growing out from a triangular area which extends slightly in front of the ears with its apex below. The mane extends back to the start of the withers — unattended it may grow a foot or more in length, particularly in mountain ponies and heavy horses. Sometimes it falls to one side of the neck, or it may divide and pass over each side. In saddle horses it is sometimes hogged, or more commonly pulled and kept at a length of a few inches, hanging free or plaited.

The ears which should be erect, actively mobile and not too large, are carried on either side of the highest point of the skull, the nuchal crest — to which is attached the ligamentum nuchae. The portion of the skull at the front and upper part of the head reaching from the nuchal crest down to the level of the temporal fossa is the cranium. This surrounds and encloses the brain (Fig. 48). The upper surface of the cranium, in front of the poll, has a midline interparietal or sagittal crest which shallows in front and diverges into the two external sagittal crests which pass down and out towards the orbits. The front wall of the cranial cavity forms part of the walls and floor of the frontal sinus (Fig. 10). This large cavity lies beneath the lower part of the forehead, and its position, depth and extent can be judged from Figs. 8 and 10. It can also be mapped out by tapping with the knuckles on the forehead between the eyes, comparing the hollow sound with that coming from surrounding more solid parts. The frontal sinus is designed to allow widening of the skull without adding to its weight. It enables the head to carry a wider upper jaw with additional space for both teeth and nasal passages. Otherwise these sinuses, of which there are two divided by a midline septum, play little part in respiratory airflow, although they do fill during expiration.

The temporal fossa is, from outward appearance, a depression on either side of the forehead immediately behind each supraorbital process of the frontal bone. This process or bridge actually completes the circle of bone forming the orbit which contains and protects the eyeball. The supraorbital process is easily detected through the skin of the forehead and can be felt throughout its length. The upper end of the mandible (the coronoid process) moves freely within the temporal fossa together with a pad of fat. Also located in the fossa, slightly raised, is the temporal muscle — whose action is to raise the lower jaw — lying on the surface of the cranium in front of the base of the ears.

The lower border of the temporal fossa, and of the orbit, is marked by a ridge of bone, felt at the outer corner of the eye, lying beneath the skin and running slightly upwards. It causes bulging of the skin and is hard to the touch. This is the zygomatic arch which completes the closing of the orbit and unites the supraorbital process of the frontal bone with the outer surface of the cranium. The zygomatic arch expands dorsally just before reaching the cranial wall, the expansion lying above the level of the temporomandibular joint between the lower jaw and the skull at the squamous temporal bone (Fig. 7). The zygoma is continued forwards in a straight line onto the side of the face as the rather prominent zygomatic ridge or facial crest. The arch and ridge give attachment to the powerful masseter muscle. This lies beneath the wide semicircular area of skin extending from below the eye to the curved hinder edge of the lower jaw where it attaches to the outer face of the mandible (Figs. 45 and 49). The temporal and masseter muscles work in collaboration in raising the lower jaw and therefore closing the mouth.

The Nostrils and Nasal Cavities

The nostril, the entrance to the nasal chamber, is a large somewhat oval opening bounded on either side by the *wings* (*alae*) (Fig. 46). These wings meet above and below to form the *commissures*; the upper being narrow, the lower wide and rounded. Comma-shaped *alar cartilages* support the wings, and these are movably articulated by fibrous tissue to the cartilage of the nasal septum which passes longitudinally down the centre of the nasal passages. This form of attachment allows movement of the alar cartilages in relation to the septum.

The cartilages provide support for the rim of the nostrils and prevent them closing during inspiration. The outer wing is concave throughout its length but the inner, while concave below, forms a convex projection near its upper end. This prominence, together with an *alar fold* passing back from it, partially divides the nostril into upper and lower parts. If a finger is introduced upwards, from below the *superior commissure*, it will enter the upper division. This is a blind pouch extending back for some four inches to the nasomaxillary notch (Fig. 10) called the false nostril. It is lined by a continuation of the skin (mainly hairless) of the face and not by the mucous membrane which covers the inner surface

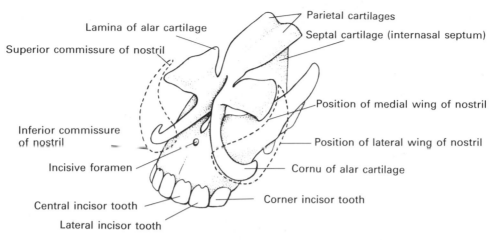

Fig. 46 Nasal cartilages and premaxillary bones.

of the nasal passages. The cartilage of the nasal septum extends beyond the apices of the nasal bones by about two inches, and gives rise to narrow parietal cartilages one on either side. Near the nostrils these plates become wider and almost fill the nasomaxillary notch in the bony wall of the nasal cavity.

About two inches from the *lower commissure* of the nostril, there is a small circular hole giving the impression that a piece of skin has been punched out. This is the lower opening of the *nasolachrymal duct* through which tears drain from the eye to the nose. Just beyond this the skin that has turned around the edge of the nostril wing is replaced by the pink mucous membrane that lines the nasal cavities.

Muscular action on the cartilages permits the nostrils to dilate and contract. They also dilate by the forcible expiration of air during the act of snorting.

The nasal bones are bilateral and triangular in shape with their bases uniting with the frontal and *lachrymal* bones, while their apices form the sharp, pointed nasal peak (Fig. 7). The two bones lie side by side and in the young animal are mainly united by cartilaginous material which becomes converted into bone later. Each is convex from side to side on its outer surface and concave on its inner. The nasal bones form the roof of the entire nasal passage. Together with the maxillary bones which form the walls, and the *hard palate* which forms the floor, they enclose the closely rolled, thin *turbinate* bones, two superimposed on either side (Figs. 10 and 48). One pair is separated from the other by the nasal septum which divides the nasal chambers into two compartments.

The Eyes

The orbit, containing the eyeball, is not placed frontally as in man but lies on either side of the forehead (Fig. 8). The eyes therefore are directed a little obliquely and do not converge upon objects lying straight ahead without some effort. The *angle of optical divergence* (the angle at which two lines of vision cross the body axis) is therefore 35½ degrees, which permits a 71 degree binocular field. Thus the two eyes see, by one means or another, through a range of 215 degrees.

It will be appreciated, then, that the horse must experience some difficulty in persuading its two eyes to converge simultaneously upon an object lying a short distance ahead. The forehead of a heavyweight hunter is much wider than that of a Thoroughbred, as a result the eyes of the latter are closer together and the possibility of both converging and focussing upon an object some little distance ahead is greater. In any event it sees no object in front clearly unless the distance from the eyes exceeds 120 cm (4 ft).

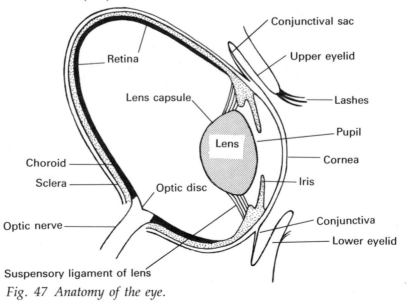

Fig. 47 Anatomy of the eye.

Horses, unlike ourselves, do not have a spherical eyeball but one which is somewhat flattened from front to back. Also the lower part is more flattened than the upper. Therefore the *retinal layer* (upon which the image is focused) is closer to the lens at the bottom than at the top. This means that both near and far objects can be in focus together. This was obviously of extreme importance in the wild. When grazing with head down, horses pursued by predators would have been able to see and focus on both food and pursuer at the same time.

Although the horse has a reasonably well-developed *ciliary muscle* the lens is non-elastic, which means that focusing is not brought about by the same mechanism as in man. In the human eye this ciliary muscle alters the shape of the elastic lens in order to focus the image on the retina. The horse must utilise movements of the head, either up or down, in order to bring the image onto that part of the retina at the right distance to ensure sharpness of image. It is probably aided in this by movements back and forth of the lens as a whole brought about by the ciliary muscles.

It is easy to tell when a horse is looking straight ahead because the two ears are pricked and the head held fairly high with the line of the forehead and nasal bones almost vertically placed − at any other time each of the eyes will discern a different picture of objects placed laterally. When jumping it is imperative that a horse's gaze should be concentrated on what lies ahead and not in other directions. For this reason, when approaching a jump, it should have freedom to hold its head in a position which enables it to view the jump to the best advantage.

As an added obstruction to vision the wide muzzle obscures view of objects below eye level. A horse is therefore unable to see anything below this from the time its head is about 120 cm (4 ft) from a jump. This accounts for an animal galloping to a jump then making a frantic effort to pull up in order to avoid a crash. The average horse has to view the jump from the start of the run-up, estimate the distance to the point of take-off, and having reached it, jump blind. This applies to showjumpers, but less to racehorses which usually take-off over a hurdle when considerably more than 120 cm (4 ft) away from it.

The upper and lower eyelids surround and enclose the *palpebral fissure*, a straight line when the lids are closed, but elliptical with its long axis upwards and outwards when the eye is open. The eyelids act as movable curtains protecting the front of the eye, the upper being larger and thicker than the lower. Opening and closing the eye is performed by the upper eyelid while the lower remains more or less stationary.

The outer surface of each lid is formed from a continuation of the skin of the face, covered by short hairs. The lower lid also has some long tactile bristles. The upper lid carries a number of thick stiff eyelashes arranged in four rows; these cross each other like a trellis but do not interlace. The lower lid carries only a few thin lashes. In both lids most lashes emerge from the centres and few from near the extremities.

The inner surface of each lid is lined by a thin, moist, sensitive membrane known as the *conjunctiva*, and is moulded so as to move freely over the eyeball. The conjunctiva is continuous with the outer surface of the *cornea*, the transparent window at the front of the eye. However the corneal conjunctiva is a layer of extreme delicacy, being only one cell in thickness, and intrinsically associated with the cornea. By lifting the lids gently from the surface of the eyeball, about 40−50 dots can be seen running the length of the inner surface of each lid. These are the *Meibomian* or *tarsal glands* which secrete an oily substance onto the edges of the lids. Tears are produced continuously from the lachrymal gland and pass over the surface of the eye to clean it. Normally these drain away down the nasolachrymal duct into the nose. The coating of oil from the Meibomian glands prevents the overspilling of tears onto the surface of the face.

The stiffness of the lids, more marked in the upper, is due to the inclusion between the skin and conjunctiva of each lid of a strip of fibrous tissue, densest along the free edge of the lid.

There is a third eyelid, the *membrana nictitans*, which lies at the inner angle of the eye with its free edge just visible. It consists of a thin, flexible, more or less T-shaped cartilage covered in front by the conjunctiva. This eyelid passes across the surface if pressure is placed on the eyeball through partly closed lids. It is not operated directly by a muscle, but the stem of the cartilage is embedded in a pad of fat which lies in the orbit by the side of the eyeball. The cartilage pushes the nictitating membrane over the eye each time pressure on the eyeball squeezes the fat outwards. It thus acts as a shield as well as a type of screen-wiper, lifting foreign materials off the sensitive cornea.

It must be understood also that the eye retracts automatically into its socket whenever stimulated by pain or threatened from the outside. This is effected by contraction of the retractor muscle which passes from the bone behind the orbit to the back of the eyeball, surrounding the optic nerve like a sheath. Contraction of this muscle pulls the eye back into the socket pressing against the fat and causing the third eyelid to cover the cornea. In cases of tetanus when the retractor muscle

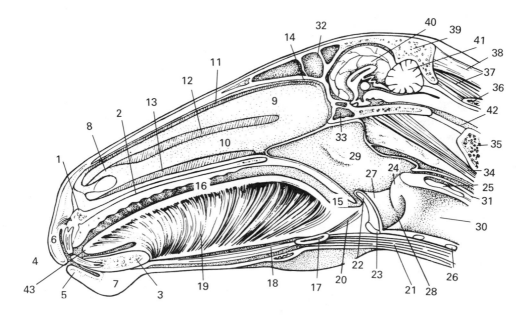

Fig. 48 Diagrammatic sagittal section of the head.
(1) Premaxilla. (2) Hard palate. (3) Mandible. (4) Incisor tooth.
(5) Lower lip. (6) Upper lip. (7) Prominence of chin. (8) Alar fold.
(9) Dorsal turbinate. (10) Ventral turbinate. (11) Dorsal nasal meatus.
(12) Middle nasal meatus. (13) Ventral nasal meatus. (14) Ethmoturbinates.
(15) Soft palate. (16) Oral cavity. (17) Hyoid bone. (18) Geniohyoid
muscle. (19) Genioglossus muscle. (20) Hyoepiglottic muscle.
(21) Sternohyoid muscle. (22) Epiglottic cartilage. (23) Thyroid cartilage.
(24) Arytenoid cartilage. (25) Cricoid cartilage. (26) Tracheal ring.
(27) Glottic margin. (28) Vocal cord. (29) Nasopharynx. (30) Trachea.
(31) Oesophagus. (32) Frontal sinus. (33) Sphenoid sinus. (34) Rectus
capitis ventralis muscle. (35) Ventral arch of atlas. (36) Dorsal arch of atlas.
(37) Rectus capitis dorsalis muscle. (38) Ligamentum nuchae. (39) Occiput.
(40) Cerebral hemisphere. (41) Cerebellum. (42) Spinal cord. (43) Tip of
tongue.

is involved in the general muscular contraction that occurs, the third eyelid remains raised and almost covering the eyeball. This is one of the most diagnostic signs of the disease.

The lachrymal gland lies within the orbit between the underside of the supraorbital process and the eyeball, above the outer corner of the eye. Several ducts open from this gland into the conjunctival sac. Tears are shed and pass across the eyeball towards a pair of lachrymal ducts close behind the free edge of the eyelids at the inner corner of the eye. These ducts empty into the nasolachrymal duct buried partly in the outer wall of the frontal sinus and nasal cavity, passing forward and downward to open in the floor of the nostril. This opening can be seen as a clean-cut orifice by dilating the nostril, as mentioned earlier.

Looking at the eye itself we can first see the cornea at the front of the eyeball, a transparent layer through which light passes. In the horse it is oval, being wider in its transverse diameter. It is fitted into the white outer layer, the *sclera*, just as a watchglass fits into a watch. Through the cornea the pigmented *iris* is visible. It is usually in the form of a dark brown curtain, sometimes nearly black, but in some odd-coloured horses may be partly white. A variable aperture is located in the centre of the iris known as the *pupil*. In horses over four years old this is oval, but in younger animals is usually rounded. At the upper border of the pupil note several black hanging bodies with probably a few more projecting upwards from the lower border, the *corpora nigra*. Sometimes these are so numerous they appear to occlude the pupil. They undoubtedly act in some way to cut down the light entering the eye, but their real purpose is somewhat obscure.

The Ears

Each ear comprises three compartments of which only the *external ear* is visible. The *middle* and *internal ears* are contained within the *petrous temporal bone* which lies laterally on the posterior end of the skull at either side. The middle ear contains the *tympanum* or *ear drum*, a thin elastic membrane situated between the external and middle ears. Sound vibrations cause this diaphragm to vibrate, the vibrations being transmitted to three small bones — the *malleus*, the *incus* and the *stapes* — within the cavity of the middle ear which are linked together. These in turn transmit the vibrations to the fluid within the ear.

The skin covering the outer surface of the ear is hairy; the inner surface carries little hair apart from that along its edges. Support for the external ear is provided by three separate cartilages lying between the layers of the skin. The main, *conchal cartilage* is somewhat trumpet shaped. Its outer orifice is elliptical with margins meeting above and below at acute angles (Fig. 45). The conchal cartilage is freely movable and capable of elevation and depression. It can also turn forwards, outwards or backwards — towards the direction of sound. At its lower end it becomes a complete tube where it overlaps the ring-shaped *annular cartilage*. This surrounds the *external auditory meatus*, a ring of bone jutting from the temporal bone and leading to the tympanum. The third cartilage, the *scutiform*, is irregularly quadrilateral in shape and lies beneath the skin of the forehead over the temporal muscles. It helps to keep the ear erect by acting as an area of attachment for muscles of the external ear (Fig. 49). Between the skin and cartilages run a number of veins, arteries and nerves. Some of the vessels are apparent through the skin, especially in Thoroughbreds.

The Lips, Mouth and Tongue

The mouth or *oral cavity* (Fig. 48) is subdivided into two parts by the teeth and jaws. The space outside the teeth is enclosed by the lips and cheeks, the mouth cavity proper lying inside the teeth. When the teeth are in contact the two parts are still connected through the *interdental space* in front, and in the area behind the last molar teeth.

The lips are two musculomembranous folds joining near the first cheek tooth. The upper lip is rounded and moulded over the incisor teeth. It is wide and fleshy and has a shallow median furrow or *philtrum*. It carries on the surface of its skin a number of long sensory hairs. The upper lip is so expansive that it can be grasped and brought forward well away from the teeth. This fact is made use of when applying a twitch to impose control for procedures such as clipping or internal examinations to which the animal may object.

The lower lip is held more tightly to the incisor teeth with less slack to spare. It carries beneath it a somewhat rounded mass, the *prominence of the chin*. This is formed by a mixture of fibrous tissue, fat and the *levator* (lifting) muscle which raises the lower lip. The lower lip however, is limited in movement, whereas the upper lip can be projected and used to nuzzle the ground or manger in search of grain or grass.

The cheeks form the sides of the mouth and are continuous in front with the lips. The internal lining of both lips and cheeks is reflected above and below onto the gums, and is reddish in colour frequently showing pigmented areas.

The tongue may be inspected by parting the lips and inserting the hand into the interdental space between the incisor and cheek teeth. The front end is free and spatulate in shape and can be drawn out of the mouth and examined. The hind end or *root* is thick and cannot be moved from its resting position. The tongue is elongated and fills the

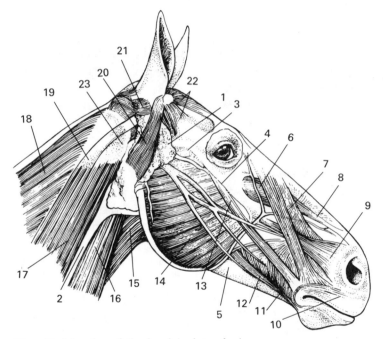

Fig. 49 Muscles of the head in lateral view.
(1) Parotid gland.   (2) Jugular vein.   (3) Zygomatic arch.   (4) Facial crest.
(5) Ramus of mandible.   (6) Levator muscle of the upper lip.   (7) Levator
nasolabialis muscle.   (8) Dorsal part of lateral nasal muscle.   (9) Lateral nostril
dilator muscle.   (10) Orbicularis oris muscle.   (11) Buccinator muscle.
(12) Depressor muscle of the lower lip.   (13) Zygomaticus muscle.
(14) Masseter muscle.   (15) Omohyoid muscle.   (16) Sternomandibularis muscle.
(17) Brachiocephalic muscle.   (18) Splenius muscle.   (19) Mastoid tendon of
the brachiocephalic muscle.   (20) Parotido-auricular muscle.   (21) Cervico-
auricular muscle.   (22) Scutularis muscle.   (23) Wing of atlas.

space between the two halves of the lower jaw in the floor of the mouth. It is a highly muscular organ, in fact practically solid muscle throughout. The tongue muscles, divided into intrinsic and extrinsic varieties, move it in a number of directions, and some originate from outside the body of the tongue from the hyoid bone (Fig. 15) and the *ramus* of the mandible (Fig. 48).

When the tip of the tongue is drawn out and raised it will be seen that its movement is somewhat limited because it is attached to the floor of the mouth by a fold of mucous membrane known as the *frenulum linguae*. On either side of the frenulum are a pair of raised *papillae* which indicate the position of the openings of the sub-mandibular salivary glands.

The mucous membrane covering the tongue is raised into papillae of four kinds:

a. *Filiform papillae*, closely packed fine, greyish structures giving a pile to the upper surface (*dorsum*).
b. *Fungiform papillae*, flattened, mushroom shaped, scattered along the dorsum and sides.
c. *Circumvalate papillae*, one on each side of the dorsal midline 12 cm (5 in) from the laryngeal opening, each surrounded by a trench.
d. *Foliate papillae*, on the dorsum and sides just in front of the anterior pillars of the *soft palate*.

The papillae are the seat of nerve endings mediating the sense of taste.

The roof of the mouth is formed by the hard palate in front and the soft palate continuous with it (Fig. 48). The hard palate is covered by a dense mucous membrane divided centrally and longitudinally by a median *raphe* which is crossed by about 18 or 20 curved ridges, their convex edges pointing forwards. It is partly concave and bounded on either side by the premolar and molar teeth. At the front the hard palate fills the interdental space between the incisor and molar teeth. In stallions and geldings over three years old there will be a canine tooth here, one on either side of the mouth. In mares the canine is usually absent or else rudimentary. The hard palate extends forward as far as the concavity behind the upper incisor teeth (Fig. 10).

The soft palate is an oblique, valve-like, musculomembranous curtain separating the mouth cavity from the *pharynx*. Its anterior (oral) surface looks downwards and fowards and is covered with a mucous membrane continuous with that of the hard palate. On each side a short fold passes down to the sides of the tongue, the *anterior pillars of the soft palate*. Owing to its length — the free border of the soft palate contacts the *epiglottis* of the *larynx* — the *common pharynx* may be regarded as being closed from the oral cavity except during the passage of food or drink towards the *oesophagus* (Fig. 48). The free border is continued on either side by a membranous fold in the pharyngeal wall, the *posterior pillar of the soft palate*. The pharyngeal wall between the two pillars of the palate is occupied by the *diffuse tonsil*.

The large size of the soft palate explains why the horse has difficulty mouth breathing, and also why it has difficulty vomiting through the mouth. If vomiting does occur, which is rare because of the nature of the horse's stomach, the ejected matter usually escapes through the nostrils.

By taking the front portion of the tongue between the lips, through the interdental space, it is possible to inspect the premolar and molar teeth using the tongue as a gag. Note the arrangement of these teeth. At birth the foal has three cheek teeth; at two years old, five; at four to five years old it has a complete set of six cheek teeth. Take note of sharp edges, uneven wear, a step mouth in which some teeth project farther than others, missing teeth, caries (diseased or decayed areas of tooth), or teeth worn down nearly to the gums.

The Facial Muscles

The *cutaneous muscle* forms a thin and usually incomplete layer beneath the skin of the face, though a supplementary sheet exists; the two components being capable of wrinkling the skin in a way that gives expression to the face. The facial muscles are concentrated around the orifices — the mouth, nostrils and eyes — and generally originate from the bones of the muzzle (frontal, nasal, maxilla, etc.).

Both the mouth and eye have surrounding *sphincter muscles* to close them: the *orbicularis oris* in the lips and the *orbicularis oculi* in the eyelids. Both also have *dilator muscles* to open them. Below the eye, between the facial crest and the outer edge of the nasal bone, there is a thin longitudinal ridge produced by the levator muscle of the upper lip. A section of this also acts as a nostril dilator, raising the outer wing of the nostril. The levator of the upper lip can raise it so that a horse exhibits all its incisor teeth with the lip fully everted. Sometimes a horse does this when it smells food, but it is most commonly seen in a stallion when he is teasing a mare.

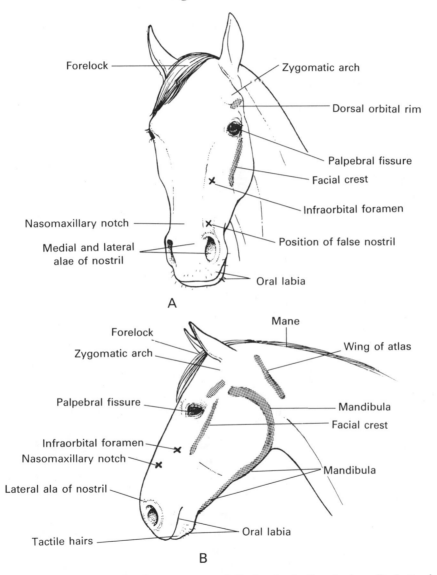

Fig. 50 Surface anatomy of the head. A. Front view. B. Lateral view.

The skin over the space between the nasal peak and the upper jaw (the nasomaxillary notch) is free and very flexible and is associated with three separate dilator muscles on either side (Fig. 49). These are attached to the cartilages of the nostril wings so that raising the skin and dilatation of the nostril at one side is synchronised.

The lower lip is provided with a *depressor muscle*, and the cheeks contain a large muscular sheet — the *buccinator muscle*, which can flatten the cheeks — thus pressing food between the teeth.

Finally the external ear has a set of superficial muscles associated with the three cartilages to which they are attached, arising from the surface of the head and neck. These can prick the ears forward or lay them back so that the ear opening faces to the rear.

The importance of all these superficial muscles, especially those of the eyelids and lips, can best be appreciated when a horse suffering from paralysis of any one of these muscles is examined.

The Intermandibular Space

This space lies below and between the two horizontal halves of the lower jawbone, the *mandibular rami*. These are felt under the skin back to the angle of the mandible and are crossed by the facial artery and vein and the *duct of the parotid salivary gland* midway between the body and the angle of the jaw. The lower edge of the mandible is thus a useful place for taking the pulse. Run the tips of your fingers along the inner edge of the bone and the throb of the pulse may be felt as the artery crosses the jaw about 8 cm (3 in) from the angle. The normal pulse rate is 35 beats per minute in the resting horse with a variation between 28 and 40. This increases rapidly with fast exercise.

In the centre of the intermandibular space, immediately below the skin, lie the *mandibular lymph glands* arranged in two elongated groups. These are the glands that become inflamed and swollen in influenza and other throat infections, and are often the seat of abscesses in strangles.

In the middle of the hindmost part of the space the larynx is palpable and joins up with the *trachea* before the latter passes down the neck (Figs. 45 and 48). Gently squeezing the trachea, especially near the larynx, will often make a horse cough. The sound of this cough may help in diagnosis.

The larynx is a short tubular structure at the junction of the pharynx and trachea — the passage leading from the nasal chamber to the lungs. It is made up of five cartilages articulated together. These serve as attachment areas for muscles which open and close the *glottis* (the opening into the larynx) by tightening or slackening the mucous membrane. The epiglottis rests in the median plane and is the most anterior of the cartilages, projecting in front of the glottis (Fig. 48).

When a horse swallows and food passes back from the mouth it must cross over the larynx to gain entrance to the oesophagus, the food passage to the stomach. The epiglottis protects the larynx by bending backwards when pressed by the tongue, so preventing food from going the wrong way. The glottis is thus sealed when food passes over it. Paralysis of the muscles activating one of the two *arytenoid cartilages* of the larynx, usually that of the left side, causes partial obstruction of the airway when the vocal fold becomes flaccid. This occurs in the condition known as *roaring*.

The larynx is suspended from the base of the skull by the hyoid apparatus (Fig. 15). The *thyroid cornua* of the hyoid articulate with the *thyroid cartilage* of the larynx, and a membrane passes between them on either side. The hyoid bone is placed at the root of the tongue and much of the tongue musculature has its origin on the hyoid apparatus (Fig. 48). Also a special projection, the *lingual process*, extends forwards from the hyoid into the body of the tongue. Through this the hyoid supports the tongue and enables it to move about in the floor of the mouth.

The Neck and Poll

Immediately behind the mandible, and following its vertical margin, is a triangular area which commences at the ear and has its base at the angle of the jaw (Fig. 45). Beneath it is the *parotid gland* and many of the large vessels and nerves supplying the head and neck. It is continuous with the *jugular furrow* which passes down the length of the neck.

The parotid gland is the largest of the salivary glands and can easily be felt as it lies almost directly beneath the skin. It commences at the root of the ear and stretches downwards filling up the space between the wing of the atlas and the edge of the lower jaw (Fig. 49). Between the skin and the outer surface of the gland is a thin layer of muscular tissue. The upper end of the parotid gland embraces the root of the ear, while its lower end is bordered by the *external maxillary vein*. Below and behind the base of the ear the parotid gland abuts onto the *brachiocephalic muscle*. The *internal maxillary vein* passes through the substance of the gland to join with the external maxillary to form the *jugular vein* at the lower and hinder corner of the gland.

The wing of the atlas lies at the extreme upper part of the neck behind the base of the ear. Its prominent rim is subcutaneous and lies a few inches below the level of the mane. In front it bounds the parotid gland while behind it a shallow furrow runs obliquely down the neck. This represents the upper border of the brachiocephalic muscle (Chart 3). This muscle is present in the neck and arm and has an important bearing on forelimb action. It is a long, flattened, rather fleshy muscle arising from the *mastoid process* of the *temporal bone* behind the ear, and also the wing of the atlas and the transverse processes of the second, third and fourth cervical vertebrae. After travelling down the length of the neck it is inserted into the deltoid tuberosity and crest of the humerus and the fascia of the shoulder and arm. When the muscle contracts it pulls the arm forwards but its efficiency depends to some extent upon the position of the head at the time. This explains why a horse moves more freely in front when the head is fully extended. It also indicates the disadvantages of riding on a tight rein and of impeding the horse by harnessing the head and neck into unnatural positions. In the neck the brachiocephalic muscle can be felt beneath the skin; its degree of development may be noted when judging a horse for fitness.

In the neck the brachiocephalic forms the upper boundary of the jugular groove, after which it passes over the front of the shoulder joint and inserts onto the shaft of the humerus. It is a powerful muscle having a two-way action. When the head is advanced and the neck held firmly by its own muscles, contraction of the brachiocephalic carries the arm and knee forwards to the maximum degree attainable. When the horse is standing still contraction of either muscle alone will help turn the head to the same side.

The *sternomandibularis* is a long and narrow muscle which extends from the sternum to the angle of the jaw (Fig. 49), forming the ventral boundary of the jugular furrow. The jugular vein is subcutaneous, and running parallel with it, but deeper in, is the *common carotid artery*.

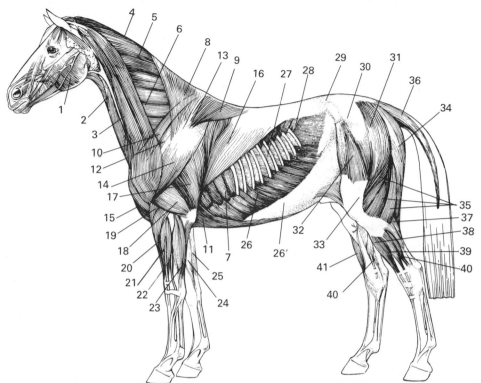

Chart 3 The superficial muscles of the horse.

*(1) Masseter.   (2) Sternomandibularis.   (3) Brachiocephalic.   (4) Rhomboideus.
(5) Splenius.   (6) Cervical part of serratus ventralis.   (7) Thoracic part of
serratus ventralis.   (8) Cervical part of trapezius.   (9) Thoracic part of
trapezius.   (10) Anterior deep pectoral.   (11) Posterior deep
pectoral.   (12) Supraspinatus.   (13) Infraspinatus.   (14) Deltoid.
(15) Anterior superficial pectoral.   (16) Latissimus dorsi.   (17) Long head of
triceps.   (18) Lateral head of triceps.   (19) Brachialis.   (20) Extensor carpi
radialis.   (21) Common digital extensor.   (22) Lateral digital extensor.
(23) Ulnaris lateralis.   (24) Flexor carpi radialis.   (25) Flexor carpi ulnaris.
(26) External abdominal oblique.   (26') Aponeurosis of external abdominal
oblique.   (27) External intercostal.   (28) Serratus dorsalis caudalis.
(29) Lumbo-dorsal fascia.   (30) Gluteal fascia.   (31) Superficial gluteal.
(32) Tensor fasciae latae.   (33) Fascia lata.   (34) Semitendinosus.
(35) Biceps femoris.   (36) Sacrococcygeals.   (37) Lateral head of
gastrocnemius.   (38) Long digital extensor.   (39) Lateral digital extensor.
(40) Deep digital flexor.   (41) Tibialis anterior.*

This is a point worthy of note, for it is not uncommon for inexperienced individuals to penetrate the jugular vein when attempting to give intravenous injections. The needle may then enter the artery with, very often, dramatic results — death is even possible.

Down the lower margin of the neck through the thin strap-like *sternothyrohyoid* muscles the trachea or windpipe is easily felt. On the left side the oesophagus lies along the upper surface of the trachea in the same plane as the jugular vein. Although the oesophagus is not readily discernible it becomes so when the horse eats or drinks and the material swallowed dilates it as it descends.

In the lighter breeds in particular, the transverse processes of the cervical vertebrae are felt on the lateral surface of the neck (Fig. 45). These are most apparent halfway down, and lie relatively low in the neck at this point. Farther up they assume a higher level but their firm substance can still be felt manually.

It is quite common for subcutaneous and intramuscular injections to be given in the neck. In doing so it is important to note the bony landmarks and make sure they are avoided when inserting a needle. Also, because of the importance of muscular tissue in athletic animals, it is wise to limit any risk of pain or stiffness after injection; muscular pain will inhibit use of the affected muscle. For this reason, intravenous injection is the least objectionable way of administering drugs to horses — as long as the drug in question can be given safely by this method.

The Forelimb

The Shoulder

The muscles in the region of the shoulder help to tie the limb to the body, there being no direct bony union here (Fig. 2). These muscles act as weight supporters and shock absorbers since practically two thirds of the body weight is carried on the thoracic limbs.

The chief landmarks in the shoulder region are:

    a. the upward rise of the shoulder away from its junction with the neck;
    b. the withers;
    c. the spine of the scapula;
    d. the point of the shoulder;

e. the sternum and pectoral muscles;

f. the triceps muscle mass.

In a well-rounded shoulder the junction with the neck is gradual and streamlined, except perhaps in harness horses in which some seating for the collar is needed. In most cases however, a collar fits a streamlined shoulder well providing it has sufficient width on either side to accommodate it.

The withers is the highest point of the thoracic spine and is formed by the dorsal spinous processes of the third to tenth thoracic vertebrae. The highest point of all is created by the fourth and fifth processes (Chart 1). The withers is held firmly in place by ligaments between the spines, and by a series of other ligaments and muscles which are attached to them. These include the funicular portion of the ligamentum nuchae (Fig. 17). The dorsal spinous processes also give anchorage to a number of muscles which greatly relieve the sharpness of the withers and help to mould the region into its general contour without undue sharpness of the spinal ridge (Charts 1 and 2). First is the flattened triangular sheet of superficial muscle, the trapezius. This originates by its base from the midline of the neck, withers and thorax, i.e. from the funicular part of the ligamentum nuchae and the supraspinous ligament back to the tenth thoracic vertebra (Chart 3). The apex of the triangular sheet is inserted into the scapular spine. Deep to the trapezius is the rhomboideus muscle which ties the scapula into the sides of the spinous processes and the ligamentum nuchae (Figs. 2 and 52). This muscle, like the trapezius, has both thoracic and cervical parts.

The division between the neck and shoulder is marked by the scapula with its overlying muscles on either side of the scapular spine. This spine is easily found beneath the skin in anything but an overfat horse; the supraspinatus muscle lies in front of it and the infraspinatus behind (Fig. 52). Both muscles insert onto the lateral tuberosity of the upper end of the humerus close to the shoulder joint. Because of the exposed position of this joint both these muscles have synovial bursae beneath their tendons of insertion. When well developed the muscles raise the level of the skin overlying the scapula. Excessive development, more common in a horse in which the scapula is upright rather than oblique, is unpopular since it is thought to cramp shoulder action.

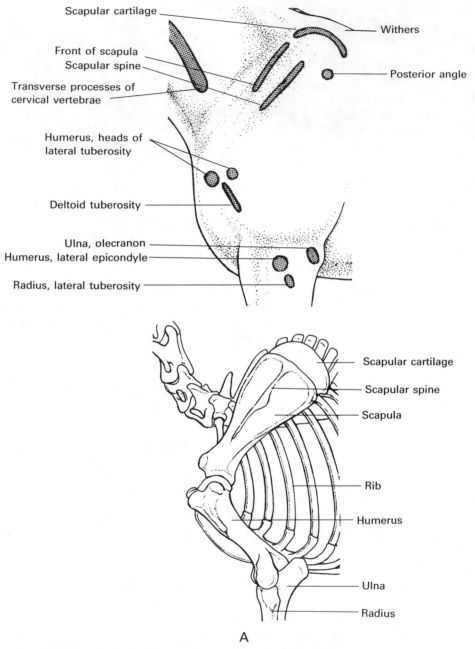

Scapular cartilage

Front of scapula
Scapular spine

Transverse processes of
cervical vertebrae

Humerus, heads of
lateral tuberosity

Deltoid tuberosity

Ulna, olecranon
Humerus, lateral epicondyle

Radius, lateral tuberosity

Withers

Posterior angle

Scapular cartilage

Scapular spine

Scapula

Rib

Humerus

Ulna

Radius

A

Fig. 51A. Surface anatomy of the shoulder.

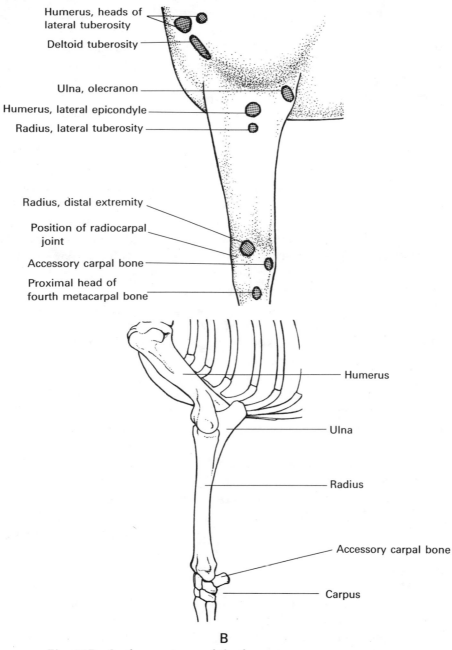

Humerus, heads of
lateral tuberosity

Deltoid tuberosity

Ulna, olecranon

Humerus, lateral epicondyle

Radius, lateral tuberosity

Radius, distal extremity

Position of radiocarpal
joint

Accessory carpal bone

Proximal head of
fourth metacarpal bone

Humerus

Ulna

Radius

Accessory carpal bone

Carpus

B

Fig. 51B. Surface anatomy of the forearm.

The scapular spine and the fascia covering the infraspinatus muscles give origin to the *deltoideus* which can be felt on the outside of the shoulder joint as it passes down onto the deltoid tuberosity of the humerus (Chart 3). The deltoid meets the brachiocephalic in front which also has an insertion onto the deltoid tuberosity after crossing, and being moulded on, the front of the shoulder.

It is important when examining the outer aspect of the shoulder to observe the degree of scapular obliquity. In other words to take note of whether the shoulder slopes backward between its two extremities, or whether it lies vertically. This degree of inclination can be accurately gauged by the practised eye, but the novice may gain a better idea by drawing a chalk line from the point of the shoulder to the upper end of the scapular spine, then another from the point of the shoulder parallel with the ground, and measuring the angle formed between the two.

It is preferable that the scapula should incline well back at its upper end enabling the horse to advance the limb and carry the knee and foot as far forward as possible. It should be noted that at the walk, however good the action may be, very few horses bring the front of the knee farther forward than a line dropped vertically from the point of the shoulder. When trotting the knee may advance to a line dropped from the poll, in canter the toes of the forefeet may reach as far as a line dropped from the nose when the head is moderately extended, but at full gallop with head outstretched the foot seldom advances to the level of a line dropped from the nose.

Endurance is not associated with an upright shoulder, and although many horses thus furnished attain speed they have to perform more work for it. Incidentally, a horse with an upright shoulder is less able to absorb concussion, and, as a result, may be an uncomfortable ride.

If we look at the shoulder area from the front we can identify the cariniform cartilage at the front of the sternum. This lies in the midline of the chest at the base of the neck. From the sternum the pectoral muscles pass downwards and outwards to converge on the humerus in the region of the crest of the greater tuberosity. The pectorals also insert onto the lesser tuberosity and into the fascia of the arm and forearm (Fig. 2). The pectorals therefore form a triangular sheet with the base on the sternum and the apex on the humerus. Of the pectoral muscle complex the *superficial pectorals* form a distinct prominence on the front of the chest easily recognisable in the living animal. The *deep pectoral* muscle is represented at the front of the chest by an anterior portion which takes its origin from the lateral surface of the anterior part of the sternum. It passes forwards and upwards over the front of the shoulder beneath the brachiocephalic towards the cranial angle of the scapula (i.e. the front angle of the bone nearest the head) on the supraspinatus muscle (Fig. 52 and Chart 3). It attaches to the fascia covering the supraspinatus and onto the scapula directly at the cranial angle. The importance of this divison will become evident later.

The front border of the pectoral muscles meets the lower border of the brachiocephalic over much of the front of the shoulder, but they separate at the *supraclavicular fossa* beside the *manubrium*, or front

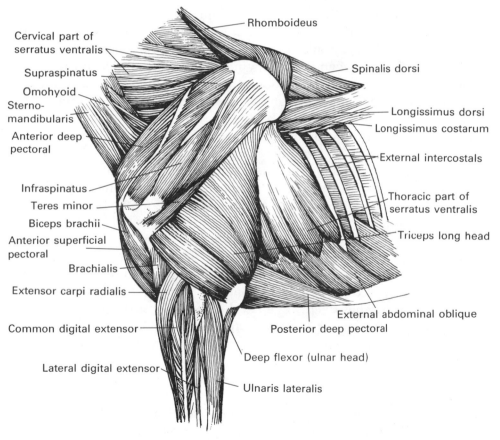

Fig. 52 Deep muscles of the shoulder and arm in lateral view.

extremity, of the sternum. This fossa is clearly palpable and is located at the lower end of the jugular groove.

At all times the point of the shoulder can be felt and seen. It is formed by the greater tuberosity of the upper end of the humerus which stands in front of the joint surface. The biceps brachii muscle passes across the front of the joint in the intertuberal groove from an origin on the scapular tuberosity. It travels downwards to its insertion into the radial tuberosity on the inner side of the head of the radius. This muscle flexes the elbow joint and extends the shoulder. It can be located as it passes down the upper arm overlying the front of the humerus (Fig. 52). Where the tendon passes over the intertuberal groove it is cushioned by a synovial bursa. This bursa occupies the most anterior and prominent site in the forelimb and is exposed to injury from bruising.

The triceps comprises three separate muscles extending between the hinder edge of the scapula and the olecranon process or point of the elbow (Fig. 52). Between them they make up the rounded muscle mass lying alongside the ribs just above the elbow joint, i.e. the triangular section that bulges just in front of the saddle flap and underlies the rider's knee or shin. The *long head of the triceps* is the largest part and it originates on the scapula; it therefore has a flexing action on the shoulder as well as an extending action on the elbow joint. The two remaining triceps' heads, the *lateral* and *medial*, are both shorter and have their origins on the hinder side of the humeral shaft. These two cross only the elbow joint and so have the sole action of elbow extension.

Another important muscle is the latissimus dorsi which lies behind the shoulder region covering the side of the chest and extending up onto the back (Chart 3). From its broad origin at the midline in the thoracic and lumbar regions the muscle fibres converge to end on the teres tuberosity of the humerus in common with the teres major muscle. This latter muscle lies deeply against the posterior surface of the scapula and is one of the major flexors of the shoulder joint. The latissimus dorsi also finds extensive insertion onto the fascia in the upper arm.

The Forearm and Knee

Both the forearm and the gaskin (second thigh) require close consideration since they act as the medium between body and earth and need to be strongly developed to stand up to the amount of work and strain demanded of them. It is worth mentioning here that primary injury to the muscles of these areas is far less common than to the greater-sized muscles higher up in both fore and hind limbs. This is an indication that the muscles of the forearm and gaskin are in constant use — because of the nature of the stay apparatus and the fact the horse is constantly on the move when grazing — and therefore strong. The greater muscles, e.g. the triceps, pectorals and brachiocephalic in front, the gluteals, semimembranosus and vastus of the hind limb, and the longissimus dorsi in the back, are mainly involved in the heavier work of trotting, cantering and galloping. They therefore are less in use and lose fitness when a horse is out of training. The higher incidence of primary injuries in these muscles — i.e. injuries that are not related to underlying bony disturbances — is an indication of the part they play in locomotion and the importance of slow work in the early stages of training to build up muscle strength. Most primary injuries are incurred when there is a greater loading on an individual muscle, e.g. when changing pace — as in acceleration — because of fatigue, or due to unbalanced movement.

At the elbow the olecranon process (the point of the elbow) is distinct (Fig. 25), and both the lateral epicondyle of the humerus and lateral tuberosity of the radius are palpable. The radius and ulna are hidden by muscles except at the lower part of the inner surface of the forearm above the knee where the radius lies beneath the skin.

The muscle mass in front of the limb from the elbow down has its origin mainly on the lateral epicondyle of the humerus and the lateral tuberosity of the radius. Contained in this are the extensor muscles of both knee and digit — the lower limb — which carry the limb and foot forward. The most important of these are the extensor carpi radialis acting on the knee and the common digital extensor acting on both knee and digit (Fig. 52). The carpal bones are only evident as a group, but over the front of the knee the extensor tendons pass in canals formed by thickened fascia and connective tissue, each tendon protected by its own enveloping synovial sheath (Fig. 53). These tendons can be distinguished manually, and their synovial sheaths often become involved in cases of broken knees arising from falls.

The muscle mass at the back of the limb from the elbow down has its origin mainly on the large medial epicondyle of the humerus and the olecranon process. Contained in it are the flexor muscles of the carpus, fetlock and digit. Included are both superficial and deep flexors as well as the carpal flexor muscles. At the outer side and back of the knee the *accessory carpal bone* can be seen and felt protruding behind the limb. A ridge on its upper surface corresponds with the insertion into it of the tendons of the *ulnaris lateralis* and *flexor carpi ulnaris*, the knee flexors. The concave inner surface of the accessory carpal helps to form the carpal canal, through which pass the tendons of the flexor muscles at the back of the knee. It is possible to feel the rows of knee bones especially if the foot is raised and they are slightly separated. The knee requires little more description, as it has been discussed previously (Figs. 26 and 27).

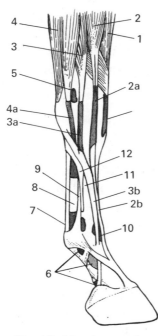

Fig. 53 Muscles, tendons and tendon sheaths of the lower part of the forelimb in lateral view.
(1, 1a) Extensor carpi radialis and synovial sheath. (2, 2a, 2b) Common digital extensor muscle, synovial sheath and tendon. (3, 3a, 3b) Lateral digital extensor muscle, synovial sheath and tendon. (4, 4a) Ulnaris lateralis muscle and synovial sheath of its long tendon. (5) Carpal synovial sheath.
(6) Digital synovial sheath. (7) Superficial flexor tendon. (8) Deep flexor tendon. (9) Suspensory ligament. (10) Synovial bursa under extensor tendons. (11) Large metacarpal bone. (12) Small metacarpal bone.

Returning to the region of the elbow, the lower tendon of the biceps brachii muscle inserts into the radial tuberosity on the inner side of the head of the radius. This upper end of the radius is covered lightly by the superficial pectoral muscle which is thin enough here to allow the tuberosity to be palpated through it. Just behind the biceps tendon the *median nerve* and the comparatively large *median artery* may be felt as they lie on the radius. Both artery and nerve can be felt by rolling them beneath the fingertip against the radial tuberosity. This makes a very convenient site at which to take the pulse, in addition to the facial artery beneath the lower jaw.

On the inner side of the forearm, at its lower third, the chestnut is located. This is a horny oval structure of uncertain origin and function.

The Metacarpus and Digit

From the knee down is a very important part of structural anatomy in ridden horses. Within its compass the principal tendons and ligaments for supporting the body and moving it from place to place are found.

The metacarpal bones, one large and two small, are mainly subcutaneous and they can be felt with ease. The lower extremities of the splint bones are unmistakeable small nodular prominences. Any bony adhesions or exostoses — splints — existing between the large and small metacarpals can be felt with ease. The metacarpal tuberosity can be felt at the front of the cannon bone, below the knee, onto which the *extensor carpi radialis* (knee extensor) attaches. Below this the *common digital extensor tendon* runs down the front of the cannon and phalanges, to pass onto the extensor process of the third phalanx within the hoof.

Behind the fetlock the proximal sesamoid bones can be felt, but as they are tightly encased in ligaments and covered by flexor tendons their detail is not easy to determine (Figs. 33 and 54). Their position is indicated by a tuft of hair surmounting a horny structure, the *ergot*, equivalent to the metacarpal pad of the dog. Immediately above the sesamoids, at the hinder part of the outer surface of the fetlock, is a small space between the tendons and the metacarpal bone. At the bottom of this space is felt the *digital artery*, pulsating; also the *volar nerve* and *common digital vein* can be rolled beneath the fingers. The artery divides into medial and lateral branches which can be felt as they pass out from the space over the sides of the fetlock.

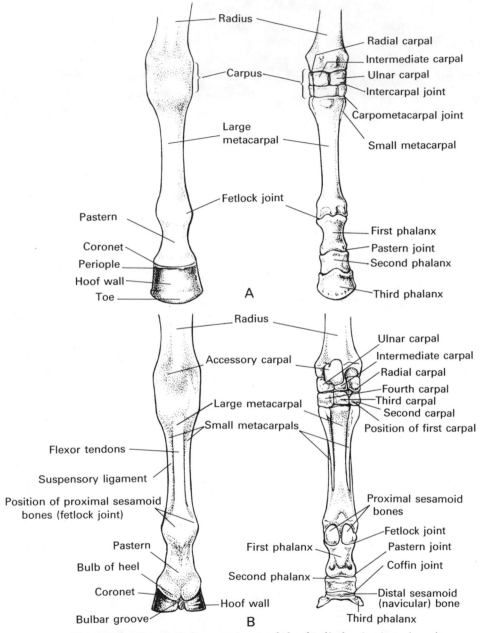

Fig. 54 Surface and deep anatomy of the forelimb. A. Anterior view. B. Caudal view.

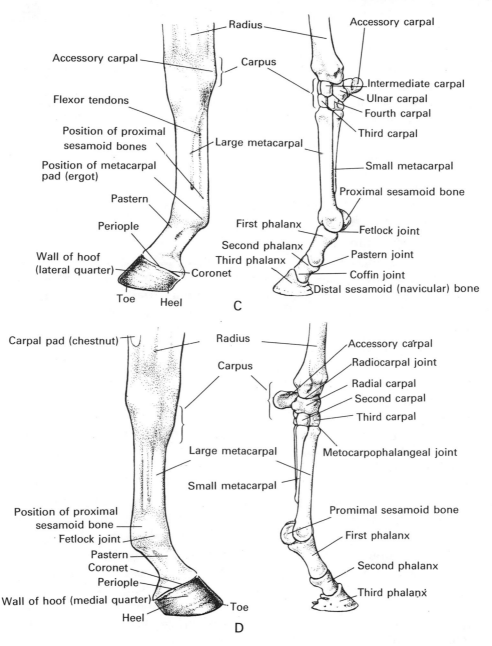

Fig. 54 C. Lateral view. D. Medial view.

The tendons of the superficial and deep flexor muscles are outstanding features here. The superficial flexor tendon begins above the carpus and is joined by a strong fibrous band, the radial or superior check ligament, which fuses with it near the carpus. It then continues down through the carpal canal in the carpal synovial sheath (Fig. 53). In the cannon region it flattens and then widens into a ring above the fetlock through which the tendon of the deep flexor muscle passes. The superficial flexor tendon divides into two parts below the fetlock, and attaches on either side of the hinder part of the first and second phalanges. Through the fork thus created, the deep flexor tendon, within the digital synovial sheath, passes on its way to be inserted into the sole of the third phalanx at the semilunar crest (Fig. 29). A bursa, the navicular bursa, is interposed at this point between the deep flexor tendon and the distal sesamoid bone.

The two flexor tendons, one overlying the other, can be felt easily, but it is not always easy to separate them by touch; neither are they the only structures existing behind the metacarpal bone, between the bone and the skin. The deep flexor tendon is joined to the back of the knee by a 10 cm (4 in) fibrous band, the subcarpal or inferior check ligament. When excessive strain falls on the deep flexor this ligament takes part of the weight and often becomes injured.

Between the deep flexor tendon and the cannon bone there is the suspensory ligament, a flat, elastic band about 2.5 cm (1 in) wide which takes origin from the back of the knee, then passes down the limb. At the lower third of the cannon it divides into two branches, one of which is inserted into the upper part of each sesamoid bone (Fig. 33). The suspensory ligament occupies the channel lying between the back of the metacarpal bone and the small splint bones, and, like the other structures behind the cannon, it is also subject to strain. Below the proximal sesamoid bones it sends two tendinous cords to travel in a forward direction to be inserted, one on either side, into the common extensor tendon at the front of the limb (Fig. 33).

It is easier to distinguish these various structures by touch if the foot is lifted and the fetlock, pastern and coffin joints slightly flexed. In any instance in which lameness arises it is better to leave the diagnosis of the affected part to a veterinary surgeon since each separate structure may require special attention. In many cases more than one of the structures may be involved. Inflammation of tendons gives rise to swelling, heat and pain. Ultimately repair of the strained and torn tendon fibres is accomplished by the natural laying down of fibrous tissue. This has a habit of contracting after union has been effected, with the result that the tendons lose their elasticity and are effectively shortened. The consequence is that some degree of fetlock flexion may occur as a permanent feature. The fetlock and foot may then assume different positions in relation to the rest of the limb and to one another. This may well lead to altered placement of the foot, and is therefore, a common cause of secondary lameness.

The Foot

With a hunter capable of carrying 75 kg (165 lb), the four feet cover a total area of approximately 600 sq cm (92 sq in) of ground. Sometimes, in movement, only one foot is making contact with the ground, at other times two or three. When a horse lands from a jump it has been estimated that the weight-bearing limb may be met with a force equivalent to many times the animal's body weight. The reality of this gives some indication of the burden imposed on the limb and the risk of injury at any point or time during exercise or competition.

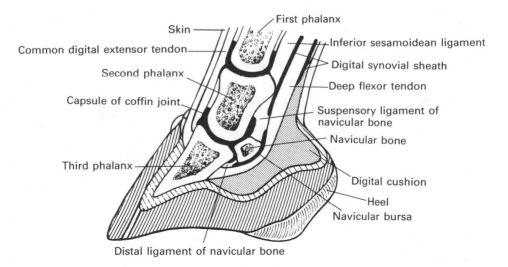

Fig. 55 Diagrammatic vertical section of the bones, tendons and hoof structures below the fetlock.

The shape of the feet varies with breed and type; the Thoroughbred tending to have smaller and more delicately designed feet, with, sometimes, light walls and upright boxy shapes. Low-heeled, elongated feet are also seen, though there is little doubt that the eventual shape of many a Thoroughbred foot is heavily influenced by the interferences of man during its early life owing to shoeing and trimming. Generally, working breeds have larger, flatter feet with stronger walls and greater durability.

Native pony breeds have tough foot construction, suited to animals which live outdoors throughout the year; kept indoors, these animals may be prone to laminitis. They tend to have hard horn in their feet and the heels are high and upright.

The wall of the foot is developed by a downward growth of horn secreted by the cells of the *coronary band*. Sometimes called the *coronary cushion*, this is a ring of modified skin, covered with papillae which carry cells capable of secreting horn. Above the coronary cushion is a narrow groove separating it from a somewhat similar but smaller cushion known as the *perioplic ring*. This secretes a layer of waterproof varnish which is intended to cover the wall of the foot in order to prevent loss of moisture with an accompanying shrinking of the hoof and hardening of the wall. The periople is often rasped off by the farrier when finishing the front of the foot, but, clearly, it is an exercise that makes little sense.

The rate of secretion from the coronary band permits the complete replacement of the horny wall in a period of 8 to 10 months. When the rate of growth is irregular, alternating ridges and circular depressions encircle the wall. The influence of diet also produces rings. When the horn growth is accelerated, as when the horse is out on spring grass, raised grass rings are produced. When horses rough it in winter, depressions in circular form may appear later. Deeper and wider circular grooves follow an attack of laminitis.

In a correctly shod foot the weight of the body falls upon the wall and frog — which should be permitted to make contact with the ground at shoe level. When only the wall receives the weight, the buffering effect of the *digital cushion*, the large pad of fibrous tissue which overlies the frog, is lost. The result is greater strain on higher structures of the leg, such as the fetlock, cannon and tendons. Limb circulation also suffers.

At the heel the horny wall bends forwards and inwards in the shape of a V to meet the hinder end of the frog (Fig. 31). The inturned wall forms an upright partition of horn and this, in company with the upright wall of the heel, constitutes the bar of the foot. The purpose of the bar is to take additional weight upon the heel. Horses, except during the slow walk, land on the heel first, then the frog, and finally the toe, as the body travels over the area occupied by the foot. (At the slow walk the foot lands virtually level.) Each time this happens the frog should take the weight, force the angle of the bars open, and prevent the heels from caving in and contracting. Each time the bars are forced apart they lift the fibroelastic digital cushion above them and exert pressure on the network of blood vessels contained within the horny casing of the foot. This helps to empty these veins of blood and drive it up into the leg, where it continues through the circulatory system of the limb.

The digital cushion extends upwards between the cartilages, one of which attaches to the wing on each side of the rear end of the third phalanx (Fig. 32). Under ground pressure the digital cushion forces these structures apart. To some extent this overcomes the contraction which would otherwise occur at the coronary band each time the lower end widens when the foot strikes the ground.

It is possible that shoeing can throw the natural functions of the foot out of gear. This is particularly so when tight nails press on the sensitive tissues and set up acute inflammation within the foot.

The foot of a Welsh pony running on the hills may not be very impressive at first glance, but it fills its purpose admirably. While a high percentage of lameness in shod horses may derive from the foot, it is unusual to find this in indigenous ponies living in their natural habitat.

The terminal bone of the foot, the third phalanx, is somewhat similar in shape to the hoof which contains it, but very much smaller. It is covered with soft, sensitive, fleshy laminae, which interleave with the horny laminae on the inner side of the hoof wall. The toe of the third phalanx is somewhat chisel-like in shape and is directed down towards the sensitive laminae on the inner side of the sole. When any undue weight falls upon the foot (as when landing from a jump), the tendency is for the toe of the pedal bone to descend slightly and exert pressure upon the sensitive sole. This pressure may bruise the related structures and cause excessive concussion to the pedal bone. It also, theoretically, creates the possibility of penetration of the sole by the bone.

The Trunk

The trunk consists basically of thorax and abdomen slung between the forelimbs in the muscular cradle in front, and rigidly attached by a bony union with the hind limbs at the rear. Its surface indicates a number of important features and areas. For our purposes we will divide it into three divisions: the upper surface of the back and loins, the chest, and the abdomen (Chart 2).

The back, loins and croup form the upper contour of the body from the withers to the sacrum. It has as its bony basis the last eleven or twelve thoracic vertebrae together with the upper extremities of the corresponding ribs, the lumbar vertebrae, the front part of the sacrum and the pelvis from croup to haunches. The contour, however, is moulded around the muscles lying above the vertebral column, between the spinous processes dorsally and the transverse processes laterally. These muscles are arranged in a longitudinal series extending forwards from the region of the croup and haunches. They attach en route to the spinous and transverse processes and the upper ends of the ribs. The longissimus dorsi is the major component and is the largest and longest muscle in the body; posteriorly it is greatly developed to form the common mass of the loins above the lumbar vertebrae. Further forwards it fills in the space between the spinous processes and ribs, the *costovertebral groove* of the back. These muscles are broadly palpable underneath a strong tendinous sheet, the *lumbodorsal fascia*, in the loins and hind part of the back. Towards the withers the *latissimus dorsi* and trapezius muscles cover the *epaxial longissimus system* (Chart 3 and Fig. 52).

The back is of primary importance because it receives the saddle and the weight of the rider as well as transmitting to the front part of the body the efforts of propulsion, which are communicated through the loins by the hind limbs. The muscles of the back therefore have the purpose, along with associated ligaments, of supporting the bony structures and maintaining their integrity.

The chest corresponds to the bony thoracic ribcage, bounded above by the withers and back, in front by the neck, on each side by the shoulder, arm and ribs, below by the sternum and behind by the abdomen. Only the hinder parts are available for examination (behind the shoulder and arm) but much of this is covered by muscle; both the latissimus dorsi and pectoral muscles cover the ribs (Chart 3 and

Fig. 52). Further back the limit of the ribcage, the costal arch, may be felt as it bends downwards and forwards from the beginning of the lumbar region to the xiphoid of the sternum (Chart 1). Even the ribcage has a superficial covering of muscles, the abdominal wall muscles which spread forwards to have part of their origins on its surface. The ribs may be clearly felt in the upper hinder portion of the chest where they will be found to be clearly separated by intercostal spaces filled with intercostal musculature.

The chest can be seen to accomplish regular, alternative movements, which are more or less extensive according to the state of respiration. These respiratory movements are especially perceptible in thinner horses, and are of two basic kinds:

   a. Inspiratory, in which the intercostal spaces are increased and the ribs rotate forwards and outwards resulting in a dilatation of the thoracic cavity, an enlargement of the lungs, and therefore an inflow of air.
   b. Expiratory, in which the ribs are brought together and rotate backwards and inwards, contracting the thorax and compressing the lungs, driving air out.

The intercostal muscles are responsible for only a part of the respiratory movements; other deeper muscles are also involved, in particular the muscular partition between the thoracic and abdominal cavities, the diaphragm.

The abdomen lies behind the costal arch, below the loins, and in front of the haunch, thigh and stifle. It is normally spoken of in terms of flank and belly (Chart 2). The abdominal wall is formed from several layers of muscle, the *external abdominal oblique, internal abdominal oblique* and *transverse abdominal*. These layers are important since they support the weight of the *viscera*. It has already been mentioned that the abdominal muscles have rib attachments. They also find attachment to the dense tendinous sheet covering the loins, and to the haunch bones, the ilia and the pubic areas of the pelvic bones. Weight pressing down on the inside of the abdominal wall is distributed upwards, forwards and backwards by these lateral abdominal muscles together with the *rectus abdominis* in the midline of the belly.

The surface features to identify are relatively few; there is a hollow in the flank just in front of the haunch, and the lower part of the flank

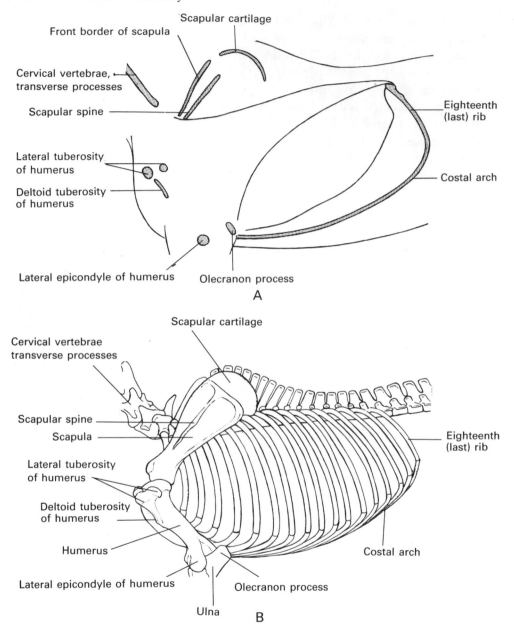

Scapular cartilage

Front border of scapula

Cervical vertebrae,
transverse processes

Scapular spine

Lateral tuberosity
of humerus

Deltoid tuberosity
of humerus

Lateral epicondyle of humerus

Olecranon process

Eighteenth
(last) rib

Costal arch

A

Scapular cartilage

Cervical vertebrae
transverse processes

Scapular spine

Scapula

Lateral tuberosity
of humerus

Deltoid tuberosity
of humerus

Humerus

Lateral epicondyle of humerus

Ulna

Olecranon process

Costal arch

Eighteenth
(last) rib

B

*Fig. 56a A. Surface anatomy of neck, shoulder and trunk, left lateral
view. B. Bones relating to the neck shoulder and trunk, left lateral view.*

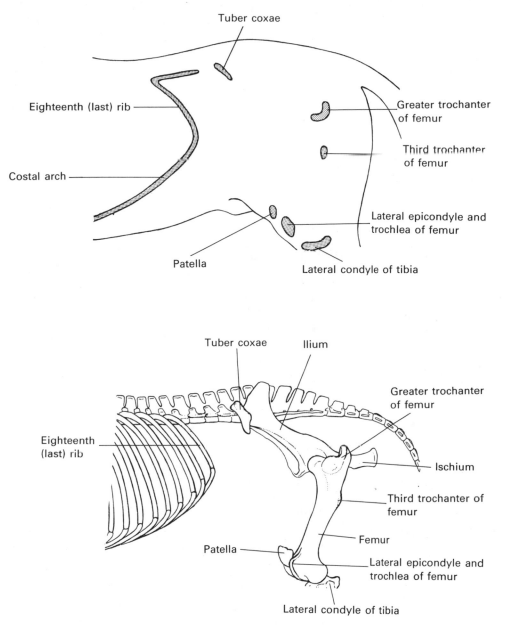

Tuber coxae

Eighteenth (last) rib

Costal arch

Greater trochanter of femur

Third trochanter of femur

Lateral epicondyle and trochlea of femur

Patella

Lateral condyle of tibia

Tuber coxae   Ilium

Eighteenth (last) rib

Greater trochanter of femur

Ischium

Third trochanter of femur

Femur

Patella

Lateral epicondyle and trochlea of femur

Lateral condyle of tibia

Fig. 56b A. Surface anatomy of the flank and quarter, left lateral view.
B. Bones relating to the flank and quarter, left lateral view.

is joined to the stifle by a very mobile fold of skin. This skin fold contains part of the cutaneous muscle which finds attachment to the patella. The lower silhouette of the belly should show a graceful curve up and back from the sternum to the groin on the inner side of the thigh. However, this curve varies with type, digestion and state of training. Horses on fibrous diets have more voluminous abdomens than those on concentrates.

The whole abdominal wall is elastic and yields to finger pressure. As it is composed of soft structures attached to the ribs, and the diaphragm forms the front margin of the cavity, the abdomen mirrors the movements of the chest in respiration.

The Hind Limb

The Hip, Thigh and Buttock

The thigh is the region where the hind limb becomes separated from the trunk. It is limited above by the haunch, croup and quarters, below by the leg and stifle, in front by the flank, and is free behind (Chart 2). The anatomical bases of this region are the pelvic bone, the femur and the associated muscles.

The chief landmarks affecting the shape of hip and thigh regions when viewed from outside are:

a. The *tuber coxae*, point of the haunch or pin bone. (The two pin bones if viewed from behind should be level. Occasionally one becomes 'knocked down' and is accordingly lower than the other.)

b. The *tuber sacrale*, point of the croup, the highest point at the rear of the horse.

c. The *major trochanter of the femur*, point of the hip, although deep can be felt from the surface.

d. The *tuber ischii*, point of the buttock or seat bone; one on either side below the tail.

e. The *third trochanter of the femur* in the upper part of the thigh.

f. The *lateral epicondyle of the femur* and the patella at the stifle.

The hindquarters extend out, back and down from the point of the croup, consisting of a mass of muscle which clothes the buttock and the outer and rear surface of hip and thigh down to the stifle and leg.

Immediately behind the croup and arising from the shaft of the ilium (and from both the tuber sacrale and tuber coxae, and the sacroiliac and sacrosciatic ligaments) is the bulk of the muscle mass which gives the haunch its rounded contour, the gluteal muscles (Chart 3 and Fig. 58). These muscles have insertions on the major and third trochanters of the femur and the femoral shaft between the two.

In front of this group is a dense superficial tendinous layer containing a muscle which is indistinguishable on palpation from the gluteal mass. It is the tensor fasciae latae and originates on the tuber coxae (Chart 3). The tendinous fascia associated with it clothes the front part of the thigh like a binding mesh and attaches to the patella and thus onto the tibial crest of the second thigh.

The hind part of the quarters is formed from a rounded muscle mass extending from the sacral and coccygeal vertebrae down the outer and hind side of the thigh to attach to the outer surface of the stifle joint. It also has attachment to both inner and outer surfaces of the tibia, and to the tuber calcis through the dense fascia of the lower leg. This muscle mass is very important and needs to be considered more closely. The biceps femoris is large and related to the hind edge of the gluteal mass, in fact a slight groove may be felt between them (Chart 3). It passes in a curved direction down the thigh covering the greater trochanter, to the lateral surface of the leg where it is readily felt from the surface. The attachment areas of this muscle are complex, so are its actions as shall be seen later. Broadly speaking three parts are present each having a different origin of insertion. The most anterior attaches to the rear surface of the femur near the third trochanter, as well as to the patella and lateral patellar ligament (Figs. 40 and 41). The second attaches to the crest of the tibia below the stifle. The third part attaches to the dense crural fascia which encases the lower part of the leg and is inserted onto the tuber calcis, the point of the hock. This part assists in the formation of the posterior contour of the limb and is associated with the tarsal tendon.

The semitendinosus muscle is long and extends along the hind border of the biceps femoris down the back of the thigh having passed over the tuber ischii en route. Thus it is distinctly palpable for much of its length (Chart 3). The muscle terminates in a wide tendon on the inner surface of the stifle joint. This tendon has attachment onto the tibial crest and the fascia of the leg, and has a part which joins with the

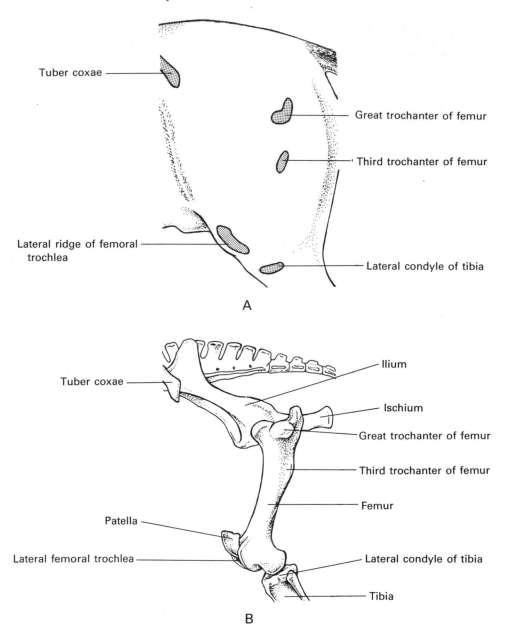

Fig. 57a A. Surface anatomy of the quarter, left lateral view. B. Bones relating to the quarter, left lateral view.

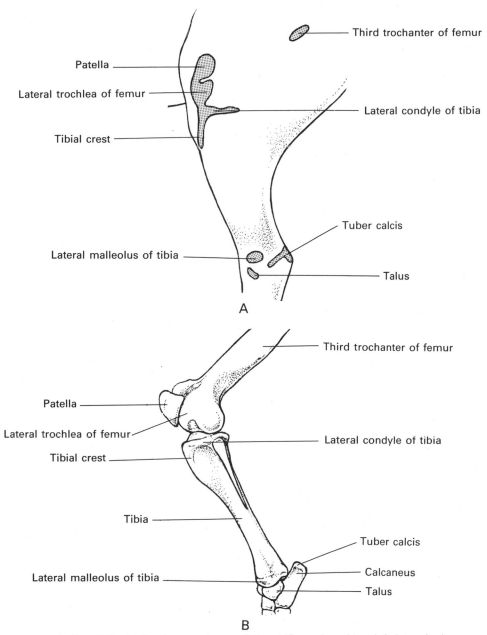

*Fig. 57b A. Surface anatomy of the stifle and gaskin, left lateral view.
B. Bones relating to the stifle and gaskin, left lateral view.*

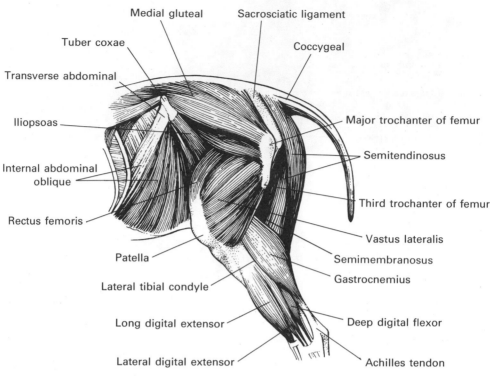

Fig. 58 Deep muscles of the hip, thigh and leg in lateral view.

tarsal tendon of the biceps femoris to terminate on the tuber calcis.

The semimembranosus muscle is the hindmost member of the quarter muscles and is only distinctly palpable at the root of the tail where it borders the pelvic outlet and where it in part covers the posterior face of the tuber ischii (Chart 3 and Figs. 36 and 58). Lower down the back of the thigh it sinks in between other muscles and attaches to the medial epicondyle of the femur.

These muscles of the hindquarters comprise the hamstring group and have basically two areas of origin. All three have deep origins from the tuber ischii, but more superficial origins extend from the dorsal and lateral sacroiliac ligaments and the first two coccygeal vertebrae (Fig. 36). These muscles are extremely important in locomotion and will be mentioned again later.

Still in the region of the buttocks notice the long flexible tail limited in front by the quarters, below by the anal opening, and by the points of the buttocks on either side. The tail has a skeleton consisting of coccygeal vertebrae (Chart 1). It also has coccygeal muscles which can elevate, depress or incline it laterally. Long hairs are present except on the lower surface at the base, and are useful in dislodging flies, etc. from the hindquarters.

The inner side of the thigh has no really distinctive characteristics, the skin being very thin and only attached to the underlying structures by loose fatty connective tissue. The greater part of the surface is occupied by the *sartorius muscle* in front and the *gracilis* behind. These are two straps of muscle which have their primary insertions through a fascial sheet onto the medial patellar ligament. The gracilis also has attachments to the crural fascia and thus indirectly onto the tuber calcis of the hock. The front of the thigh is composed of the four parts of the *quadriceps femoris* muscle (*rectus femoris* and the tripartite *vastus*) deeply palpable through the skin and fascia lata (Fig. 58). This group of muscles covers the front and sides of the femur. The origins are from the ilium and the femur, but all four parts insert onto the patella. The patella is attached through the three patellar ligaments (Figs. 40 and 41) with the tibial crest and tuberosity. These structures can be felt clearly at the front of the stifle joint. The patellar ligaments are to be regarded as the tendons of the quadriceps muscle which communicate the action to the tibia, the patella being included as a sesamoid bone. In the region of the stifle the musculocutaneous fold from the flank passes on to the front surface of the limb (Chart 3).

The Gaskin and Hock

The muscles of the leg cover almost all of the tibia except its inner face which is subcutaneous. In great measure these are concealed in the upper part by the lower ends and tendinous insertions of the quarter muscles. Below the stifle the tibial crest is easily identified and the shaft of the bone can be felt throughout its length. As in the forearm the muscles fall into two major groups. The muscle mass in front of and on the outer side of the limb from the stifle down (the gaskin or second thigh) has its origin from the extensor fossa of the femur and the lateral condyle of the tibia. These are the digital extensor and hock flexor muscles, and may assist in stifle joint fixation. The *long digital extensor* arises from the extensor fossa at the lower end of the femur, and lies just below the skin at the front of the second thigh giving it visible contour (Fig. 58). It can be located and felt easily. It ends in a long tendon which passes over the front of the hock within a synovial sheath. Below the hock it is joined by the tendon of the *lateral digital extensor* to form a *common extensor tendon*. This passes down in front of the metatarsal bone to the third phalanx, to be inserted into the extensor process (Figs. 29, 33 and 59).

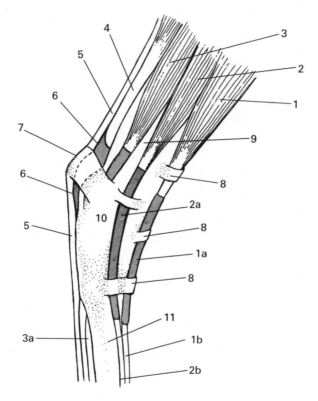

Fig. 59 Muscles, tendons and tendon sheaths of the hock in lateral view.
(1, 1a, 1b) Long digital extensor, synovial sheath and tendon.
(2, 2a, 2b) Lateral digital extensor, synovial sheath and tendon.   (3, 3a) Deep flexor and tendon.   (4) Gastrocnemius tendon.   (5) Superficial flexor tendon.
(6) Synovial bursa under superficial flexor tendon.   (7) Tuber calcis.
(8) Annular ligaments.   (9) Tibia.   (10) Tarsus.   (11) Metatarsus.

Beneath the long digital extensor, between it and the tibial shaft, lies the *tibialis anterior* muscle. This hock flexor is composed of ordinary muscle tissue with fibres arising actually from the tibial shaft. At the lower end of the tibia it is succeeded by a tendon which divides; one part is inserted into the head of the metatarsal bone, the other into the fused first and second tarsal bones of the hock.

We are already aware that hock flexion is synchronous with stifle flexion and that when one of these joints extends the other does likewise. A muscle which has an important bearing on this reciprocal mechanism is sandwiched between the long digital extensor and the anterior tibial muscles. It is the tendinous, cord-like *peroneus tertius* (Fig. 5) which arises from the lower end of the femur in common with the long digital extensor. In its course down the leg it rests on the tibialis anterior muscle. Immediately above the front of the hock the tendinous cord bifurcates; one branch is inserted into the head of the metatarsal bone, the other into the fourth tarsal bone of the hock. The action of the tibialis anterior is to flex the hock. The tendinous peroneus tertius plays a purely mechanical role; it synchronises the action of the stifle and hock ensuring that the hock flexes when the stifle flexes. It is on this account that a horse with a straight stifle also has a straight hock and one with a bent stifle also has a bent hock. As already said, in a horse possessing a normal stifle and hock, a line dropped perpendicularly from the tuber ischii passes down the back of the hind limb from hock to fetlock.

The muscle masses at the back of the limb from the stifle down (Fig. 58) have their origin on the lower end of the back of the femur (the supracondyloid ridges and fossa), and the upper end of the back of the tibia. These areas are not palpable from the surface, being deeply covered by the lower ends of the thigh muscles, and the crural fascia. The muscles are stifle and digital flexors and hock extensors. The outline of the posterior part of the leg is formed by the belly of the *gastrocnemius* muscle — halfway down, the powerful tendon of this muscle begins. It is intimately associated with the tendon of the deeper-lying superficial flexor muscle which is itself almost entirely tendinous. This combined tendon is palpable as a very stout cord, the *Achilles tendon* (Figs. 58 and 59). The gastrocnemius tendon attaches to the tuber calcis, while the superficial flexor tendon broadens and flattens to cap the tuber calcis, attaching to it but then continuing down behind to the underside of

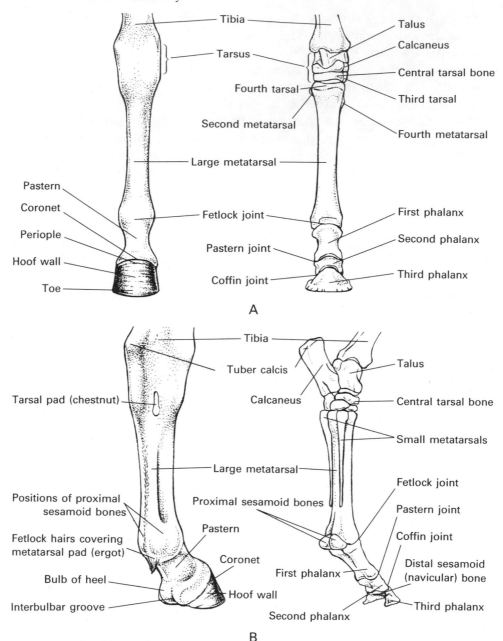

Fig. 60 Surface and deep anatomy of the lower hind limb. A. Anterior view. B. Caudal view.

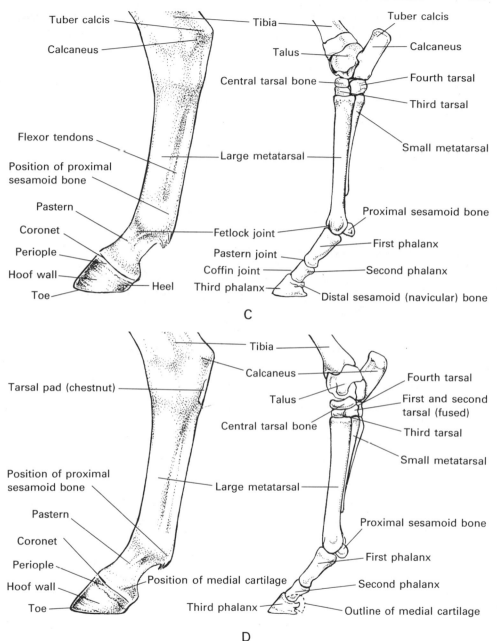

Tuber calcis
Calcaneus
Flexor tendons
Position of proximal sesamoid bone
Pastern
Coronet
Periople
Hoof wall
Toe
Heel

Tibia
Talus
Central tarsal bone
Large metatarsal
Fetlock joint
Pastern joint
Coffin joint
Third phalanx

Tuber calcis
Calcaneus
Fourth tarsal
Third tarsal
Small metatarsal
Proximal sesamoid bone
First phalanx
Second phalanx
Distal sesamoid (navicular) bone

C

Tarsal pad (chestnut)
Position of proximal sesamoid bone
Pastern
Coronet
Periople
Hoof wall
Toe

Tibia
Calcaneus
Talus
Central tarsal bone
Large metatarsal
Position of medial cartilage
Third phalanx

Fourth tarsal
First and second tarsal (fused)
Third tarsal
Small metatarsal
Proximal sesamoid bone
First phalanx
Second phalanx
Outline of medial cartilage

D

Fig. 60 C. Lateral view. D. Medial view.

the foot. Another entity of functional significance is a strong tendinous band associated with the gastrocnemius muscle passing from the femur to fuse with the tarsal tendon of the hamstring muscles. The deep flexor muscle lies close to the hind border of the tibial shaft; its tendon, running in a synovial sheath, is felt deeply in the lower half of the leg in front of the Achilles tendon (Fig. 59).

The hock joint requires little more description other than that already given. The inner lip of the trochlea of the talus can be felt as can the medial malleolus of the tibia just above it. The calcaneus bone can also be felt from the outer surface with the prominent lateral malleolus of the tibia. The tuber calcis with the attached Achilles tendon is easily palpable, but of the other tarsal bones none is individually identifiable.

The Metatarsus and Digit

In the metatarsus, just as in the metacarpus, the third metatarsal bone is practically entirely subcutaneous except at the back. Other features are closely comparable to the forelimb. The surface features which are palpable behind the cannon bone are the borders of the suspensory and the deep and superficial flexor tendons. A check ligament, the subtarsal ligament, joins the deep flexor but is not so well developed as its equivalent in the forelimb. It is similarly a tendinous band detached from the tarsal joint capsule and attached to the deep flexor tendon.

The features of the digit below the fetlock are comparable to those of the forelimb.

7   The Horse at Rest

The general outline of structural anatomy, and the way this influences movement, has now been mapped out. To recap:

a. There is no clavicle and the forelimbs are attached to the trunk by muscle and ligament only.

b. The forelimb bears most of the concussion — as best visualised when a horse lands from a jump.

c. The head and neck act as a freely balancing, highly motile bob-weight at the front end. The neck gives attachment to muscles vital to extension of the forelimb.

d. The spinal column has only slight lateral and limited dorso-ventral movement in the area between neck and tail.

e. The thorax and abdomen together form an almost rigid trunk whose only role in locomotion is to give attachment to muscles involved in projecting the animal forward.

f. The hind limb is attached directly to the pelvis and spine by bony union. This affects the transference of hind limb kinetic forces through the spinal column.

g. The reciprocal apparatus of the hock and stifle is intimately involved in the driving force of the hind limb, and also plays a part in concussion absorbtion.

Add to these:

h. The proprioceptive reflexes, involved in normal locomotion, righting the animal and balance, all have their centres of origin in the spinal cord and brain.

Equilibrium and the Centre of Gravity

The centre of gravity varies with the individual horse, and also with its attitude at a given moment. Equilibrium of the body when at a standstill can only be maintained if a line dropped through the centre of gravity meets the ground within the oblong produced by joining up the positions of the four feet. The head and neck, as bob-weight, influence its location: when the head is lifted, the centre of gravity moves backwards; when it is lowered its location moves forwards. The ability to lift a foot off the ground and still maintain balance will depend on the relationship of the three remaining feet to the centre of gravity.

The position of the centre of gravity in the stationary horse is located on a line stretching from the point of the shoulder to the point of the buttock – tuber ischii – behind the junction of front and middle thirds of the body. It is influenced by conformation and by the length and

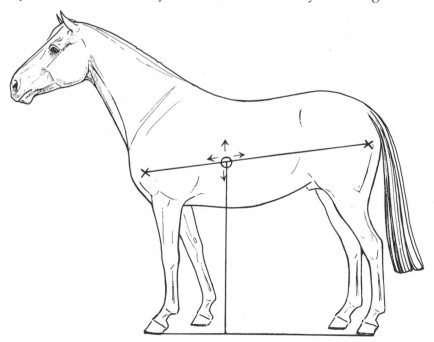

Fig. 61 Centre of gravity showing potential displacement. Arrows indicate centre of gravity moving backwards and forwards on axis (ringed).

weight of each part of the animal. It will thus be noted that the centre of gravity lies nearer the shoulder than the hip; it is estimated to lie two-thirds of the distance between hind and forelimbs. Because of this, when standing quietly at rest, a horse can lift one of its hind feet off the ground and still maintain balance. In fact horses have a habit of resting hind feet alternately, allowing the fellow limb to support the body on what is a three-point suspension. This is because the basic oblong of support can be subdivided into two triangles by lines joining the right forefoot with the left hind foot and the left forefoot with the right hind foot. This implies that when the right hind foot is lifted the centre of gravity lies within the triangle formed from the right forefoot, left hind foot and left forefoot. The opposite is true when the left hind foot is raised.

The front half of the body is a good deal heavier than the remainder as the position of the centre of gravity shows. Thus the amount of weight resting on either forefoot is greater than that resting on the hind feet. If a horse weighs 500 kg (1,100 lb), approximately three-fifths of the weight, viz. 300 kg (660 lb), is supported by the two forefeet, collectively. If one foot is lifted from the ground while the head is lowered, as when the horse is grazing, the whole 300 kg (660 lb) may be transferred to the remaining forefoot. In order to lift a forelimb and still maintain balance a considerable amount of this frontal weight must be transferred back until the centre of gravity lies behind the intersection of the diagonals of the feet. This shifting of weight within the body can be brought about by several methods.

a. Raising the head and neck.
b. Contracting the serratus ventralis muscles attaching scapulae to ribs. When both contract together they raise the thorax relative to the forelimbs (the thorax can move independently, up and down between the limbs) which may have a slight effect on the centre of gravity. More importantly, if they contract singly the weight is shifted away from the midline towards the limb on the side of the acting muscle. However, this shifting cannot occur by unilateral serratus action alone, it must be accompanied by contraction of the thoracic parts of the rhomboid and trapezius muscles of the same side. These muscles pass from the upper end of the scapula, the cartilage

of prolongation and the scapular spine to attach to the mid-dorsal line of the body in the region of the supraspinous ligament and ligamentum nuchae (Fig. 2); they can also roll the thorax over towards the scapula at the same time as it is being raised. In effect this procedure allows the thorax to be raised slightly on the side on which the muscles are acting throwing extra weight onto the forefoot of the same side, thereby taking enough weight off the opposite forelimb to permit the elbow joint to flex and the limb to be advanced.

c. Contraction of the anterior deep pectoral muscles extending from the sternum to the prescapular fascia will raise the thorax relative to the limbs, acting in a manner similar to the serratus ventralis muscles, also resembling these in their unilateral action.

d. Flexion of one or both hocks with the hind feet planted firmly on the ground.

In a similar manner the centre of gravity may be moved forward by lowering the head and to some extent by flexing a knee. However, knee flexion is not generally practised for any purpose other than establishing or maintaining a gait, since it seriously reduces the power of support and may precipitate a fall.

The Horse at a Standstill — the Stay Apparatus

The foregoing points show that the technique by which voluntary redistribution of weight is achieved — by contraction or relaxation of limb muscles, combined with perfect synchronisation of them all — is as essential when standing still as when the animal changes from standstill to walk.

It is important to consider in detail how the horse stands and why it is able to rest in the standing position with little fatigue. The reason is associated with what is termed the stay apparatus, present in both fore and hind limbs (Figs. 62 and 63).

This apparatus, in essence, consists of a system of muscles and ligaments that can lock the main joints firmly in position and hold them so until unlocked. At least part of the system is identical in fore and hind limbs, and is based on the suspensory ligament running

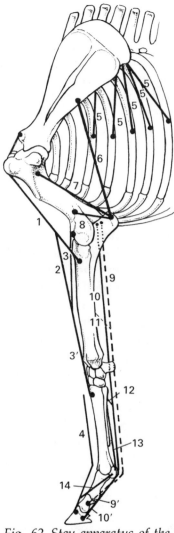

Fig. 62 Stay apparatus of the forelimb.

(1) Biceps brachii muscle.   (2) Lacertus fibrosus.   (3) Extensor carpi radialis muscle.   (3') Conjoint tendon of extensor carpi radialis and lacertus fibrosus. (4) Common digital extensor tendon.   (5) Fibrous intersections in serratus ventralis muscle.   (6) Long head of triceps muscle.   (7) Lateral head of triceps muscle.   (8) Medial head of triceps muscle.   (9) Superficial flexor muscle. (9') Tendon of superficial flexor.   (10) Deep flexor muscle.   (10') Tendon of deep flexor.   (11) Radial check ligament to superficial flexor tendon. (12) Carpal check ligament to deep flexor tendon.   (13) Suspensory ligament. (14) Extension of suspensory ligament onto extensor tendon.

down the back of the cannon bone, often termed the suspensory apparatus. The suspensory ligament divides into two branches inserted into the proximal sesamoid bones — which are themselves attached by ligaments to the first and second phalanges (Fig. 33) — and is prolonged forward on either side of the joint to join the common digital extensor tendon in front. The sesamoid bones have an action, similar to the patella, on the fetlock joint; the suspensory ligament being purely an elastic cord which serves as the main support for the joint preventing excessive dorsiflexion (overextension). The fetlock joint is normally overextended when supporting the body weight. The prolongations of the suspensory ligament to the front would appear to be a mechanism to tie down the common digital extensor tendon, acting in a similar way to the annular ligaments present in the region of the carpus and hock (Figs. 53 and 59). The suspensory ligament also serves to limit concussion and control the action of the fetlock during movement.

Supplementing the suspensory ligament are the superficial and deep flexor tendons, which are attached to muscle bodies, and not, therefore, purely supportive in the same way as a ligament. However, they do act similarly to ligaments at the limits of their extension when the check ligaments come into action to support the tendons. These check ligaments do not run, as do normal ligaments, from bone to bone, but from bone to tendon, making the tendon function as a ligament by cutting off the muscular attachment above. The superficial flexor tendons of both fore and hind limb receive a check ligament above the knee or hock (from radius and tibia respectively), and the deep flexors receive another from below the knee or hock — these coming as extensions of the joint capsule below each joint.

Thus the limb below knee and hock is supported by three elastic ligaments at the back:

a. *Suspensory ligament*, supporting the fetlock and pastern joints.
b. *Superficial flexor tendon*, supporting the fetlock and pastern joints, is musculotendinous in the forelimb, but mainly tendinous in the hind limb. The flexor tendons are limited by check ligaments and when the fetlock moves down, the joint is automatically supported by the check ligament and the tendon.

c. *Deep flexor tendon*, supporting the fetlock, pastern and coffin joints, and, like the superficial flexor tendon, equipped with a check ligament.

The suspensory ligament and the two flexors operate in series. As the body weight presses down through the fetlock this joint moves down, the suspensory ligament tightens first followed by the superficial flexor and then the deep flexor tendons.

Thus far the stay mechanism extending from the knee or hock to the foot has been described. The remainder of both fore and hind limbs is maintained in an extended position by a system of muscles.

In the forelimb the thoracic part of the serratus ventralis muscle is the major factor attaching the limb to the body (Fig. 62). Its muscular belly is interspersed with inelastic fibrous tissue which supports the body when the muscle is relaxed. This means that the weight of the body is hanging from the upper end of the scapula and it tends to flex (close) the shoulder joint. But an arrangement exists to prevent shoulder flexion, composed basically of the biceps brachii muscle which extends from the scapular tuberosity to the radius. It is largely tendinous (inelastic) in nature and tension builds up in it as the shoulder tends to flex. However, this action can only occur if the biceps is prevented from flexing the elbow joint. Two arrangements exist to prevent this flexion:

a. Both deep and superficial flexor muscles have humeral heads originating from the medial epicondyle of the humerus. This epicondyle is a relatively large projection providing a lever arm to remove the line of action of the muscles away from the centre of rotation of the elbow joint (Figs. 25 and 62). The humeral heads of both muscles are marked by much inelastic material. The normal standing position involves dorsiflexion of the fetlock joint which tenses the digital flexors, the inelastic parts are stretched and passive tension is built up in them to maintain elbow extension.

b. The long head of the triceps muscle is attached to the olecranon process of the ulna from an origin on the posterior border of the scapula. Isometric contraction of the triceps is a key factor in the shoulder/elbow fixation mechanism.

Shoulder flexion is also prevented by isometric contraction of the supraspinatus muscle which is a major shoulder extensor attaching to the medial and lateral tuberosities of the upper end of the humerus (Fig. 23).

The knee is the final forelimb joint in this process and in its normal position it is predisposed to effortless weight bearing since the radius and large metacarpal bones are in the same vertical line. It is prevented from buckling forward by an inelastic tendon inserted onto the large metacarpal bone. This is the lacertus fibrosus tendon, arising from the biceps tendon in the upper arm and running through the extensor carpi radialis muscle of the forearm. Thus tension built up in the biceps is transmitted through this system to assist in the fixation of the knee in extension.

In order to understand the stay mechanism of the hind limb (often referred to as the reciprocal system) we must try to correlate the overall structure of this limb with that of the fore limb. In the latter the scapula slopes forward and down to its junction with the upper arm at the shoulder, as the femur does to its junction with the gaskin behind. These two segments are the parts which actually connect the substance of the limb to the body. The humerus slopes back to the elbow joint, as the tibia does to the hock in the hind leg. From these points the legs are similar, the hind leg descending directly to the ground, the foreleg descending with an added joint, the knee, maintained unbent when the stay mechanism is operating.

The serratus ventralis muscle of the thorax has no equivalent in the hind limb since behind there is a bony attachment of limb to body. The biceps brachii has its equivalent in the peroneus tertius muscle, an entirely tendinous strand extending from the extensor fossa of the femur to the upper end of the large metatarsal bone (Figs. 5 & 63). Weight acting downwards tends to flex the stifle, and this is in part counteracted by tension in the peroneus tertius – its action on the stifle is reflected by a purely mechanical flexing of the hock. An arrangement exists to prevent the hock from flexing through the gastrocnemius muscle which is attached to the tuber calcis from an origin on the lower end of the femur (this muscle is only an active extensor when the foot is off the ground). When standing, the muscle is a passive extensor of the hock since incorporated into it is a tendinous band which combines

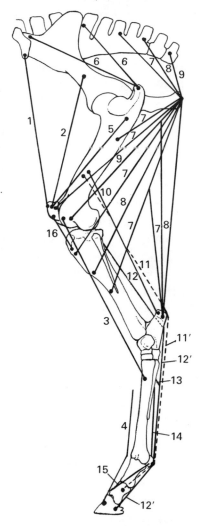

Fig. 63 Stay apparatus of the hind limb.
(1) Tensor fasciae latae muscle.   (2) Rectus femoris muscle.   (3) Peroneus
tertius muscle.   (4) Common digital extensor tendon.   (5) Vastus muscles.
(6) Gluteal muscles.   (7) Biceps femoris muscle.   (8) Semitendinosus muscle.
(9) Semimembranosus muscle.   (10) Gastrocnemius muscle.   (11) Superficial
flexor muscle.   (11') Tendon of superficial flexor.   (12) Deep flexor muscle.
(12') Tendon of deep flexor.   (13) Tarsal check ligament to the deep flexor
tendon.   (14) Suspensory ligament.   (15) Extension of suspensory ligament
onto extensor tendon.   (16) Patellar ligament.

mechanically with the almost entirely tendinous superficial flexor muscle. During standing it relieves the constant strain otherwise imposed on the gastrocnemius and maintains the hock in extension.

The overall action is one of purely mechanical opposition between the peroneus tertius and the system formed by the superficial flexor and tendinous part of the gastrocnemius. This means that should the tibialis anterior muscle contract to flex the hock, the reciprocal system will flex the stifle, and should the gastrocnemius muscle contract to extend the hock, the reciprocal system will extend the stifle as well. The horse cannot flex or extend the stifle without the hock following suit.

In order for this reciprocal action to function adequately in the standing position the stifle must first be fixed in an extended position. This could theoretically be brought about by contraction of the quadriceps femoris muscle group which inserts onto the tibia through the patellar ligaments and patella. However, a strong contraction of the biceps femoris and semitendinosus muscles (the major components of the hamstring group), as they attach to the patella, will fix the stifle in the standing position with no detectable contraction of the quadriceps femoris muscles. The biceps femoris with attachments to the back of the femur and to the patella will extend the hip joint and pull on the patella sliding it up the femoral trochlea. The patella and the medial patellar ligament may then engage with the upper end of the inner trochlear ridge and become locked in position, the stifle consequently being locked by the straight patellar ligaments in an extended position (Fig. 41B). The greater the weight then falling on the limb at the head of the femur the greater the tendency to flex the hip and the tighter is the lock. In this situation little or no muscular effort is required to maintain posture. In order to unlock the system, the quadriceps femoris mass may contract, lifting the patella, while the biceps femoris contracts to pull it laterally off the ridge. Contraction of the tensor fasciae latae muscle may also assist in the unlocking mechanism by lifting and pulling the patella laterally.

The importance of the fascia, the dense connective tissue which surrounds and binds the muscles, especially in the forearm and second thigh, has not yet been specifically mentioned. This fascia confines the muscles thus directing their actions; also it may become organised into distinct areas for binding tendons in the region of joints. This is found in the annular ligaments which bind the extensor tendons and the peroneus tertius and tibialis anterior muscles to the front of the tibia, hock and metatarsus. Finally the fascia may act as a tendon of muscle attachment, especially noticeable in the gaskin where the tarsal tendon of the biceps femoris and semitendinosus muscles attaches to the tuber calcis, this tendon being modified fascia. Likewise, the tendinous band running along with the gastrocnemius muscle, and having an important role in the reciprocal mechanism, is formed from modified fascia and is incorporated into the tarsal tendon above the hock. The fascia then plays an important part in giving assistance to the constant strain imposed on the muscles of the limb.

It must not be thought that the ability of these muscular combinations to convert four motile limbs into solid props, or relax them rapidly, is governed by voluntary muscle control alone, nor that these changes are brought about entirely automatically. Balance is a complex matter with central nervous system control, operated through proprioceptive centres in the brain and pathways in the spinal cord. The reflexes involved in stance are thought to operate at local and central levels and are subject to control from centres in the brain. Thus, a great deal of normal movement is subject to local reflex action, as when a horse walks, trots or canters. However, when an obstacle appears and has to be negotiated the local reflexes are subject to specific information that comes through the eyes to the brain. This is then fed along the cord to influence the reactions of the limbs. It should be appreciated that all these processes are fostered by muscular development and training.

The newborn foal, an hour or two after arrival, will be able to stand up and follow its mother without the training a human infant would need before doing the same thing. This suggests that ability to stand goes more readily with four limbs than with two. It could, however, be argued that while the human infant has to learn voluntary muscle control, the foal comes into the world with a capacity for reflex or automatic limb control which can only be possessed by a four-legged animal, or at least by one which does not have to maintain a two-legged stance. The human infant has first to learn how to straighten its body, with its highly flexible spine, and maintain its rigidity. Then it can learn to use its limbs. The foal has an almost rigid body, and it would appear easier to maintain balance on four limbs so long as the standing position is maintained.

When the foal starts to follow its mother both the fore and hind limbs have to move forward and, in addition, synchronise; this they achieve in most instances. This indicates a centre in the brain in charge of locomotory procedure, and also suggests a highly developed system of local spinal cord reflexes.

The whole process of movement through a series of gaits is too complicated to be acquired within hours of birth. There is little doubt that the foal's ability to assess the position of various parts of its body, and relate to both space and surrounding objects, plays a considerable part in its ability to stand and feed from its mother. The righting reflexes particularly come into play when it raises its head to get at the teat. Very often it will lose balance and fall back initially, but strength comes with colostrum and progress is marked in the first hours of life, suggesting that muscular strength comes with feeding, adding to the natural capacities of the spinal system.

Fig. 64 A foal is delivered at a higher level of development than that of a newly born human infant.

Foals are carried for rather a lengthy period in their mothers' wombs and are delivered in an advanced stage of development. A human baby is carried nearly as long, but is delivered in a less-developed state, and needs a considerable period of extra-uterine development before attaining anything like the activity and perception encountered in a newly born foal.

While the stay mechanism must be of help, collapse could not be avoided if the muscles failed to maintain a state of contraction. This suggests that a moderate degree of contraction must be maintained during rest in both extensors and flexors of the shoulder, elbow, hip and stifle joints. Modern information indicates that this is controlled at spinal level. But the foal in its early days of life does require more recumbent rest than at any stage during the rest of its life, because here the pattern is feed and sleep, feed and sleep as it gathers strength. This would suggest that the natural benefits of the stay mechanism are aided by growth and development.

8   The Horse in Motion

Moving Off

Although a foal is able to stand soon after birth, it may be slow to get out of its straight-limbed position and move one forefoot in front of the other at the walk. An adult horse has long since learned the trick of moving off from a standstill, but for a foal the matter is not immediately so easy. It has to discover how it can move its forelimbs only by adopting a special attitude or by making some kind of movement which raises the weight and liberates the joints so that they can move freely and in a straight line.

As we have already seen, the adult horse effects the forelimb freedom by a variety of means, all directed towards shifting the centre of gravity backwards. The weight which originally fell upon the forefoot is transferred to the hind foot, or feet. The actual degree of movement necessary to effect this transfer is very slight and not at all obvious. Even when an almost imperceptible hock flexion occurs and the tail end of the body sinks an inch or so towards the ground, it may release anything between 50 and 100 kilos from a forefoot and transfer it to the hind feet.

In order to lift a forefoot the shoulder and elbow will first have to flex. Shoulder flexion is brought about by contraction of several muscles, notably the deltoid, teres minor and teres major. The latter two insert on the humerus from an origin on the posterior border of the scapula (Fig. 52). Flexion of the elbow joint is brought about by biceps muscle contraction acting through its own insertion onto the upper end of the radius, together with contraction of the brachialis muscle which has an origin from the humerus and an insertion on the radius together with the biceps. At the same time the triceps muscle is relaxing, permitting the biceps to assume supremacy. The knee moves forwards and upwards thus raising the foot from the ground, while simultaneously the flexors at the back of the limb contract to flex the knee and digital joints. The foot is now suspended from the withers through the dorsal scapular ligament (arising from the third, fourth and fifth thoracic spines and attaching to the scapula along with the rhomboideus muscle), and the tendinous middle part of the trapezius attached to the scapular spine. These together support the whole forelimb when the foot is off the ground and the limb is hanging.

The limb must now be brought forward (protracted), mainly by the action of the brachiocephalic muscle and the thoracic part of the serratus ventralis muscles. The latter pulls the upper end of the scapula down and back, while the former pulls the lower part of the humerus forwards. After the limb has advanced sufficiently it is straightened again. The shoulder joint is extended mainly by the action of the supraspinatus muscle; the elbow joint is extended by triceps action on the olecranon process of the ulna. The carpus moves into extension as do the coffin, pastern and fetlock joints by contraction of the carpal and digital extensors. The coffin and pastern joints appear to overextend (dorsiflex) at the last moment, by the action of the common digital extensor. This contraction causes a build up of tension in the superficial and deep flexor tendons and their check ligaments. As backward movement (retraction) of the leg begins, the common extensor slackens and the elastic rebound of the superficial and deep flexor tendons aligns the coffin and pastern joints in their contact (impact) position with the ground. No active flexor muscle action is apparently required for proper hoof placement, elastic rebound of the flexor tendons against the common extensor tendon being sufficient.

At the moment of impact of the foot with the ground — which is virtually flat contact at the walk — the forelimb has already been somewhat retracted and is in an extended position with none of the joints undergoing rotation, the limb being rigid. The real work begins now because the body has to pass over the limb while the leg remains fixed to the ground at the foot, and the limb from the elbow to the ground remains rigid. (From here on when we talk of limb retraction we are implying rather that the body is being protracted [moved forwards] in relation to the limb which is fixed to the ground.)

The mechanism of the forward movement of the limb may be likened to a wheel in which the shoulder is the rim, the limb below it the spoke, and the foot resting on the ground the hub. The action is dependent upon the foot being able to plant itself firmly on the ground, over which it must not slip. In other words the spoke must be solidly attached to the hub. If the foot failed to maintain its hold on the ground either because its frog was inefficient, its shoe highly polished, or the ground itself wet and slippery, the leg would slip backward. But when the foot can grip the ground securely it acts as a fixed fulcrum, and in this case the impetus of the body turning above it actually drives the body forwards.

Once the foot is on the ground and carrying weight, the shoulder and elbow are fixed by the simultaneous contraction of the biceps and triceps (extensor and flexor). Backward movement of the limb, or the propulsive phase, is brought about by the contraction of several extrinsic muscles moving the forelimb as a rigid frame rotating around the muscular attachments of the scapula to the thorax. Thus the latissimus dorsi and the major part of the deep pectoral muscles pull the humerus back, while the cervical part of the serratus ventralis, the rhomboideus and the anterior deep pectoral pull the upper end of the scapula forwards (Fig. 52). These actions rotate the body forwards on the lever arm provided by the rigid leg, the fulcrum being the attachment of the hoof to the ground.

The actual propulsive force applied to the body occurs after the limb has passed the vertical, i.e. when the horse's shoulder has travelled onwards past the level of the foot. During limb retraction back to the vertical − the first half of the individual limb stride − the kinetic energy (energy derived by virtue of motion) of the impact force and the weight of the body exerting a downward force on the limb, are absorbed by several anti-concussion and weight-supporting mechanisms. Kinetic energy is stored as potential energy of displacement and reappears as kinetic energy during the second half of the limb stride where it imparts forward momentum to the body. This release of energy within muscles which have come under tension aids in joint extension.

At the moment of contact with the ground, the centre of gravity − through the tendinous thoracic part of the serratus ventralis muscle − tends to pull the scapula down and back, which in turn pulls the humerus towards the vertical. The tendency for the shoulder joint to close (flex) is resisted by the tendinous biceps muscle in front, and the inclination for the elbow to flex is resisted by the triceps muscle behind. Thus, just as in the standing position, the strong pull of the triceps and the elastic resistance of the biceps aid the stabilisation of the elbow joint during propulsion. We have then a system pivoting on an axle at about the mid-point of the upper arm which provides for smooth energy conversion. At impact the movement is down and back thus creating kinetic energy as potential energy of displacement of the scapula and humerus in the biceps, triceps, rhomboideus and cervical part of the serratus ventralis muscles (evidenced as increased tension in these muscles). The angle behind the shoulder joint flexes by up to 20 degrees between impact and when the limb is vertical due to this mechanism. As the limb passes the vertical it is no longer solely a weight supporter but becomes a propulsive strut and much of the weight is taken off it. Thus the energy-absorbing mechanism reverses in direction and gives up its stored energy which aids in shoulder and elbow extension, together with active contraction of the extensors of these two joints.

These actions of joint extension, together with the action of the extrinsic limb retractor muscles, means that the limb is used as an extensible propulsive strut by the muscles extending the joints, and as a propulsive lever by the muscles moving the limb as a whole.

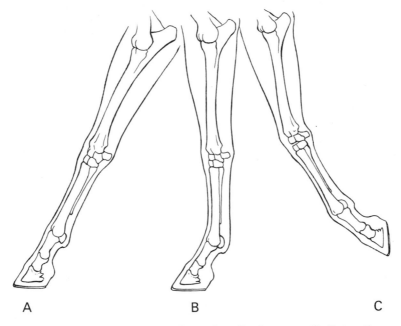

A   B   C

Fig. 65 The forelimb in: A. Extension, B. Support, C. Retraction.

When the forefoot accepts weight, the point of the fetlock sinks towards the ground. This movement is suitably checked, first by the suspensory ligament inserted into the sesamoid bones; then by the superficial flexor tendon inserted into the back of the first phalanx; next by the deep flexor tendon inserted into the third phalanx; lastly by the pull of the check ligaments inserted into the tendons of the superficial and deep flexors. This is a mechanism to reduce shock but mainly to add smoothness to the action. The fetlock is extended so that the phalanges are in a straight line with the leg when the foot contacts the ground. It then overextends as the body weight comes onto the limb and recovers after the leg has passed the vertical. By this process the limb is shortened and lengthened and this helps to keep the body at nearly the same level throughout the stride.

The action of the fetlock joint straightening from the dorsiflexed position after weight is removed from the limb provides another important source of forward propulsive thrust by adding this joint to the movement. When considering the stay apparatus we saw that as the fetlock sinks towards the ground it is supported by the three structures at the back of the cannon bone, the suspensory ligament and the superficial and deep flexor tendons. Upward and forward fetlock movement is aided by the natural elasticity of the suspensory ligament; in addition kinetic energy is stored as potential energy of displacement in the flexor tendons and reappears as kinetic energy to move the fetlock. Most importantly the powerful deep flexor muscle pulls the third phalanx back with such energy that rotation of the coffin joint and upward movement of the fetlock imparts considerable propulsive action to the limb.

When the hoof leaves the ground at push-off, the triceps relaxes and the elastic rebound of the biceps tendon pulls the lower end of the humerus forward. At the same time the rhomboideus and the cervical part of the serratus ventralis muscles are relaxing permitting elastic rebound of the tendinous thoracic part of the serratus ventralis. With these mechanisms the process of swinging the limb forward is begun.

We can now consider briefly how a horse starts off from a standstill when emerging from a starting gate or galloping away from the spot on which it has been standing. It gives a sudden push with both hind feet against the ground. In some instances the backward and downward movement of the hind feet may be so impulsive it amounts to a stamp.

The quantity of propulsion resulting will depend a great deal upon the ground surface; if it is greasy or slippery from rain or ice, the horse may not move forwards at all. The backward force is thus limited by the surface as well as by the weight of body to be shifted.

It may be noticed that this sudden stamp upon the ground causes an uprising of the front end of the body, almost as though the horse contemplated rearing. The thrust is made against the ground at the rear, but the weight of the body and its inertia at the time causes the animal's front to lift. This lifting throws weight onto the hind feet, with the result that the hocks flex, together with the stifles. When the horse again pushes its hind feet against the ground the hocks and stifles straighten, together with the hips, and the body is propelled forwards. As the forefeet are by now off the ground, they cannot assist in propulsion, so the body continues to move forwards and upwards according to the force exerted behind. An animal preparing to accelerate rapidly without raising its front feet must start by moving the centre of gravity fowards, towards the shoulders and away from the hips, in order to generate a maximum drive.

The push against the ground by both hind feet is effected by the hamstring muscles (biceps femoris, semitendinosus and semimembranosus) together with the gastrocnemius and deep flexor, and the quadriceps femoris group of muscles exerting their pull on the stifle through the patella and patellar ligaments. If the ground beneath the hind feet is firm and unyielding, the force exerted upon the lower limbs by the sudden straightening of hips, stifles and hocks will have the effect of raising the body. In other circumstances the feet may skid backwards and the forelimbs come to earth again to restore balance.

So far sufficient information has been given to enable us to look more closely at two important attributes of muscle action, both involving a concept that might be called 'co-operative antagonism'. On contraction of the limb muscles movement of the body as a whole may or may not occur. When movement does occur the muscles involved must be able to accelerate and slow the action. When movement does not occur these same muscles must exert forces which will balance the natural forces present (both horizontal and vertical) and thus prevent rotation of the levers bringing about movement.

From this it is clear that as long as the animal is not lying down the muscles of the limbs are in constant action to maintain the standing position or to bring about movement. Therefore, to keep the forelimb rigid, nervous reflexes must be operating between the shoulder extensors (biceps) and the elbow extensors (triceps). As well as their other major actions the biceps opposes flexing of the shoulder by the triceps, and the triceps opposes elbow flexion by the biceps. At the same time the biceps is actively aiding the extensors of the knee through the lacertus fibrosus and extensor carpi radialis tendon, which are resisting the flexors of the knee and digit both superficial and deep.

Many of the above-mentioned muscles which co-operate in standing must, during movement, be antagonistic to one another. During limb retraction, for instance, the limb is straightened at all the joints. Shoulder extension is brought about in part by triceps relaxation, but mainly by the biceps using muscular action and elastic recoil to extend the joint. The triceps referred to here is the long head of the triceps originating on the scapula. At the same time as this is relaxing to allow the shoulder joint to extend, the two short heads of the triceps from the rear of the humerus are actively contracting to extend the elbow and aid in shoulder extension by mechanical action through the biceps. During shoulder and elbow extension the long head of the triceps does not simply relax, it eases off in its contraction allowing the biceps to obtain supremacy, but still exerting sufficient resistance to prevent the joint from being straightened too suddenly. Were it not for this type of reflex antagonism, the joints might dislocate, the ligaments being torn by overextension of the joints. It is this synchronisation of muscles on either side of a limb which makes smooth operation of a joint a practical possibility. Accurate timing of the opposing action is also essential, for in its absence large bones like the humerus or femur and small bones like the proximal sesamoids, the navicular bone or even the second phalanges, could be completely shattered.

Coming to Earth

When the early antecedents of today's horse lived wild on the marshes they managed well on four digits per limb, although possibly only three made contact with the ground. They then had expandable footpads which kept them from sinking in the mire. The single digit of the modern horse would have been no advantage then, partly because the diameter of the sole is greater than the pastern and this would have made it difficult to extricate a foot once submerged in mud.

There are certain mechanisms in the limbs which serve to absorb weight both during normal standing and when the foot contacts the ground during movement. The horse in motion normally drops its weight on the heel first — though this varies considerably — but at rest the weight is taken mainly on the wall and frog. In the standing position body weight goes down through the limb bones to the tip of the third phalanx. This contacts the inner surface of the sole just in front of the apex of the frog (Fig. 29). Normally, injury to the sole is prevented by the presence of the laminae which attach the bone to the inner wall of the hoof. These are minute plates attached to the periosteum of the third phalanx, which interleave with similar laminae on the inner surface of the foot wall. The laminae help to absorb shock, and

Fig. 66 Landing sequence of forelimbs after jumping.

also spread the weight from the quite small area of the sole in front of the frog to the frog and wall. The sole of the foot is concave and mostly raised from the ground by shoeing; but it is not hard to imagine the strain on the third phalanx by the constant pull on its periosteum.

When a horse lands from a jump one forefoot comes to the ground first, usually making contact at the heel. As the body travels over the stationary foot the quarters and toe come into ground contact. The sole is able to descend slightly without incurring injury which not only safeguards it but also plays a useful part in limiting the effects of concussion. At impact the heels expand; weight moving down through the limb presses the second phalanx down and back against the digital cushion which in turn presses the frog against the ground. The cushion is compressed and expands on either side against the cartilages of the third phalanx spreading further the thin walls of the quarters (the digital cushion can only be fully efficient when the horny frog is able to make contract with the ground). The cartilages now move outwards and compress the coronary plexus of veins pumping blood up the limb. At the same time blood is partially held in the vascular plexus within the foot by the pressing of the cartilages against the coronary plexus. This forms a hydraulic cushion of blood for the third phalanx which also combats concussion.

All the limb joints are constructed in a way designed to protect them from injury in the normal course of events; the yielding of the shoulder and elbow joints on impact has already been mentioned. Direct concussion to the coffin joint is partially avoided by distributing weight from the second phalanx to the navicular bone, and thus onto the third phalanx. The navicular is supported by the deep flexor tendon, and the greatest pressure between these two structures occurs when the body weight passes over the foot and the fetlock is moving down towards the ground rotating the coffin joint. At the fetlock the suspensory apparatus helps change the path of the concussive forces upwards and additional support is afforded by the flexor tendons. The carpal and hock joints both function as mechanical shock absorbing mechanisms.

The Next Step

We will now presume that our foal has found its feet and is capable of advancing a forelimb and setting its foot firmly on the ground. Its natural instinct, and the need to form a three-point suspension, will induce it to advance the diagonally placed hind foot, and now a rearrangement of the centre of gravity is unnecessary. The action of the hind limb resembles that of the forelimb in that the leg is protracted and brought to the ground from which point it serves as a rigid spoke until past the vertical at which stage joint extension occurs.

Hind limb protraction is brought about initially by flexion of the hip joint which will carry the femur and stifle forward. Despite what is often said about movement of the femur, the range, in reality, is very limited because it is restricted by the heavy muscles and close attachment of the thigh to the body, limiting the length of stride. The hip flexors are in the main deep-lying muscles running from the underside of the lumbar vertebrae onto the upper end of the femur (e.g. psoas minor and iliacus). Some superficial muscles also have a flexing action, notably the superficial gluteal, sartorius and tensor fasciae latae.

When the hip is flexed the stifle is also flexed by the action of parts of the biceps femoris and semitendinosus muscles which have insertions onto the tibia in the region of the tibial crest and tuberosity. In turn this stifle flexion will bring about hock flexion through the mechanical action of the peroneus tertius. In addition, contraction of the tibialis anterior muscle will bring about hock flexion directly and stifle flexion indirectly; this occurs through the tendinous cord of the superficial flexor and the tendinous part of the gastrocnemius connecting the tuber calcis with the lower end of the femur. The superficial flexor at the same time mechanically flexes the digit. Unlike the forelimb, the superficial flexor of the hind leg is almost entirely tendinous and therefore serves a largely passive, ligamentous role.

Fig. 67 Landing sequence of hind limbs after jumping.

After the limb has been advanced sufficiently the stifle commences to extend through the action of the quadriceps femoris group of muscles. The reciprocal mechanism through the tendinous superficial flexor and tendinous cord in the gastrocnemius extends the hock joint simultaneously. The digit also extends as the extension of the hock in some measure relaxes the superficial flexor tendon. The common digital extensor muscles act in the same manner as those of the foreleg already described.

The hip-stifle-hock system means that when the foot contacts the ground the hind leg is locked like a rigid spoke. Retraction is begun by contraction of extrinsic muscles of the quarters and thighs: the biceps femoris, semitendinosus, semimembranosus and part of the gracilis pull the limb backwards by their attachments to the back of the femur and tibia, and through the tarsal tendon to the tuber calcis of the hock. At the same time, by the insertion of the biceps femoris onto the patella, they strongly stabilise the stifle joint, and thus the hock, through the reciprocal mechanism. Muscles of the rump, the middle gluteals, also turn the limb on the head of the femur, extending the hip joint. Muscles of the second thigh, especially the gastrocnemius, pull on the tuber calcis together with the biceps femoris.

The limb is thus retracted and as it approaches the vertical the stifle and hock flex slightly subserving shock absorbtion and storing up kinetic energy as potential energy of displacement of the femur. The femur therefore moves towards the vertical without moving the weight of the hindquarters against gravity. The fetlock sinks towards the ground just as in the forelimb. As soon as the limb passes the vertical the potential energy of displacement is reconverted back into kinetic energy which aids extension − through quadriceps femoris action on the patella, and rump and hamstring muscles extending the hip, stifle and hock joints with considerable power. The hock also extends through the reciprocal system and by active contraction of the gastrocnemius muscle supplementing the major pull on the tuber calcis by the tarsal tendon of the biceps femoris and semitendinosus. The deep flexor muscle is large and powerful and is the main component involved in the active straightening of the fetlock joint, whilst at the same time aiding in straightening the hock.

When the leg is fully extended, a taut line runs down from the tuber coxae to the stifle, the tensor fasciae latae muscle acting as a check to prevent overstretching of the leg joints. As soon as the hoof clears the ground at the end of the limb stride, the peroneus tertius/tibialis anterior system, by elastic rebound, snaps the hock back into semiflexion along with the stifle through the reciprocal system. The limb is then ready to be brought forward again.

We therefore have a situation which is comparable to the shoulder/elbow system, acting on the rigid limb. The quadriceps femoris and peroneus tertius function like the biceps brachii; the biceps femoris and gastrocnemius function like the triceps. However, in the hind limb, muscular co-operation is simpler since much of the action is purely mechanical. Nervous impulses pass to the stifle extensors, the quadriceps group, which are resisting the stifle flexors, the biceps femoris and semitendinosus. The latter are acting mainly on the hock which cannot be flexed as long as the stifle remains extended, owing to the mechanical tendoligaments of the peroneus tertius and superficial flexor. This relieves the strain which would otherwise be imposed on the gastrocnemius muscle and maintains the hock extended. The hock is also helped in this by the passive action of the gastrocnemius; active contraction of this muscle aids in hock extension when the limb is off the ground and not supporting weight. Co-operative antagonism is evident from the above, and is also seen during movement of the limb. Thus when the gastrocnemius is doing its utmost to extend the hock, as in the final phase of protraction before the foot meets the ground, the tibialis anterior is exerting sufficient resistance to prevent the joint being too violently straightened.

At this point we may digress a little to discuss muscle action in more general terms. The majority of muscles produce results by acting on two or more bones across a joint and tending to move one member of the joint on the other. The distribution of weight on the bones thus results in them being used as levers. However, when movement is not required, these same muscles must exert forces which balance the other forces present and prevent the levers from rotating. In many instances limb muscles are applied along the length of the limb, lying practically parallel with the lever arm. This may explain why, in the region of the joints, various projections (tuber calcis, olecranon process) and extra bones (patella, sesamoids) exist. These remove the power arm further from the centre of rotation — the joint — thus increasing the mechanical advantage at which the muscles work. This means that the force exerted by muscular contraction is increased as the line of action is moved away from the axis of the joint, though the speed of action diminishes. The muscular force thus applied is not necessarily equal to the resulting force of action, in fact the object of the lever system is that a small force applied at the end of a long lever can be made to produce a much greater force near a fulcrum.

In the case of the tuber calcis the leverage provided by the muscles making up the Achilles tendon (biceps femoris and semitendinosus through the tarsal tendon, the gastrocnemius and superficial flexor) is sufficiently great to aid in the propulsion of the animal's heavy body into the air. The lever in this instance is one in which the fulcrum is the foot in contact with the ground; the weight bears downwards on the hock and the muscular pull is applied to a rod, the tuber calcis, which projects behind and above the joint. The whole digit acts as a single lever. The same happens in the forelimb through the olecranon process and the triceps muscle.

There is a limit to the speed at which muscles can contract, thus the speed of the action which is mediated is also limited. A larger muscle, or several extra muscles acting around the same joint, will increase the power available but not the speed of movement. With the system of levers as described, the foot moves very much faster through space than the tuber calcis or olecranon process transmitting the power. The longer the lever arm then the more power is produced. On the other hand the longer the cannons and pasterns the lever of speed increases, and, relatively, the lever of power shortens lessening power and increasing speed. From this it would appear that a short, strong gaskin, with hocks high, a long cannon and straight hind pastern, should provide greater speed than if the hock were low and the cannon short. However, on the contrary, a longer cannon demands long flexor tendons and suspensory ligaments, more inclined to stress and strain, and possibly more liable to result in ultimate breakdown than when the distance between the point of the hock and the fetlock is shorter.

The Walk

Walking on four legs, after the body has been set in motion, is a matter of placing the correct foot in the right place to prevent the animal from tumbling over. For complete balance, at least three feet must be on the ground at all phases of movement and the centre of gravity must fall within the triangle created by the supporting feet. The following sequence of limb movements ensures this; LH denotes left hind, etc.:

LH LF RH RF

The sequence starts with the LH, as propulsion primarily comes from behind — a stride being defined here as a full repetitive cycle of limb movements (Fig. 68).

(We are now advised that the horse, like the human, is left- or right-handed. However, the suggestion is that greater power is generated with a right-hind lead, although scientists are not yet decided as to whether this is a phenomenon of training or a natural inclination to right-handedness.)

Each foot in the above sequence must now be lifted as soon as the one preceding it contacts the ground. As a general rule, each time a

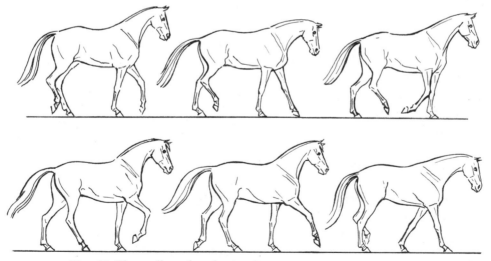

Fig. 68 The walk: a four-beat gait.

hind foot comes to the ground the quarter of that side sinks a little, the hock and stifle flexing slightly, and the way is now clear for a forelimb to move forward. The foot movements can be summarised as follows:

  a. A forefoot can be lifted when the centre of gravity lies behind the diagonal joining the other forefoot with the hind foot of its opposite side.
  b. A hind foot can be lifted when the centre of gravity lies in front of the diagonal joining the other hind foot with the forefoot of its opposite side.

Three-point suspension is only employed during the slow walk when the basic conditions for stability are the same as those applying to the stationary horse. This limb sequence is also the only one enabling a slowly moving horse to stop at any instant without falling over.

Change of Gait

During the slow walk, therefore, the horse is supported on a three-point base, with three feet on the ground at any particular moment and the fourth raised. It thus follows that the centre of gravity now lies within a triangle formed by drawing lines to pass through the three feet touching the ground. It is only when this system is effective that the horse can pull up without risk of stumbling. The fourth foot is raised and independent of the stay apparatus which gives the limb rigidity when asked to support weight.

The speed of the walk increases with the frequency of the limb movements. This implies that the length of time a limb is in contact with the ground decreases, both the total time it is in contact with the ground and relative to the time it is suspended. Thus the pattern of the faster walk demands that each foot be lifted before the foot following it actually touches the ground. The three-point suspension of the slow walk has to give way to a situation in which at times only two feet are in contact with the ground. The body is alternately supported by both limbs on one side, and then by a pair of diagonal limbs; the situation in the normal walk.

During two-point suspension the body rolls or tips slightly forward during the brief failure of support, but its equilibrium is restored when the next descending foot touches the ground. The period of two-point suspension is always followed by one of three-point. Thus during the normal walk there are momentary periods of instability.

The speed of the walk can be further increased and as soon as the time required for limb protraction equals that for retraction there will be only two limbs on the ground at the same time. With further increase in the duration of protraction there can be periods when only one foot is on the ground. Now, the longer the limbs are off the ground relative to when they are on the ground, exerting a forward thrust, the faster the horse is propelled. However, the retractor muscles work well below their maximum power output when moving slowly, and increased speed is brought about by an increased output from them.

The Trot

When the gait changes from walk to trot there is a carry-over of the two-point suspension pattern, the essential feature being that the two supporting feet are diagonals (Fig. 69). In a fully synchronised trot a forelimb and its diagonal hind limb work together to thrust the body forwards. As the speed increases the tendency is for only one foot to be on the ground at any time. With horses engaged in harness-racing the camera often catches phases in which all four feet are off the

Fig. 69 The trot: a two-beat diagonal gait.

ground with the horse still trotting. Thus there is a period during which the body is in the air with no feet on the ground; it returns to earth onto the other diagonal feet, which repeat the movement. The only real difference between the tracks left by a walking and trotting horse lies in the interval between the feet, i.e. the length of stride. All that keeps a fast trotter on its feet is the ability to place the right foot in the right spot at the right time. If anything impedes the limb movement such as a stumble or some sudden interruption, the diagonally situated foot is unable to make the necessary correction in time. When the risk is foreseen the best chance lies in a calculated change of action of the other limb on the same side, but unless the stumble occurs when the foot of this limb is actually off the ground the prospect of saving a fall is greatly lessened.

If a horse is trotted, or in fact walked, on soft ground it may be observed that the imprint of the hind feet actually overlaps those of the forefeet, i.e. there is a danger of interference between fore and hind feet. This is avoided because the forefoot is raised before the hind foot reaches the ground. If the forefoot is even a fraction late in raising, the footmarks would not overlap and the inner toe of the hind shoe might strike the heel of the forefoot. This is a common cause of overreaching. Incidentally, while on the topic of interference, the stifle joint must also be able to clear the side of the abdomen when it is brought forward.

Fig. 70 The pace: a two-beat lateral gait.

Outward rotation occurs as the hip flexes, and this in turn brings the stifle outwards and helps it clear the side of the flank.

A proportion of trotting horses are apt to exaggerate the bilateral suspension phase of the walk rather than the diagonal, with the result that they rack or pace according to the type of action they favour (Fig. 70). (The rack, or single-foot, is in fact a four-beat gait, not a two-beat gait.) The pace is more precarious than the trot since the centre of gravity tends to be shifted from side to side imparting a rolling effect to the body. However, it does have the advantage of there being no interference between fore and hind feet. The pace therefore illustrates well the bilateral phases of instability, leading to side to side oscillations of the body as it is supported alternately by right and left leg pairs. For speed to be built up with the least expenditure of energy this oscillation must be damped, and damping is largely performed by bringing the feet as near as possible to the mid-line of the body. In a fast gallop the footprints lie in a true line.

The general belief that the forelimbs provide support, serving to keep the horse on its feet, while the hind limbs provide propulsion is not wholly true. While the hind limbs keep the body moving at a speed no greater than the limbs themselves can retract, the forelimbs play a very great part in driving it forward. This is particularly so when the shoulder is obliquely placed and therefore capable of providing a longer forward extension. It is also increased when the forearm is long thus creating a longer spoke for the hypothetical wheel. In the hind limb, on the other hand, a long tibia, with a low hock and possibly a short cannon, shorten the lever arm and involve extra angulation of the stifle and hock, with the result that the hind foot comes too far behind the body.

To produce optimum results the toe of the hind foot should rotate on the ground through an arc commencing just in front of the perpendicular and for a short distance behind it (Fig. 71). The drive is then applied directly to the hindquarters and through the spine to the forequarters.

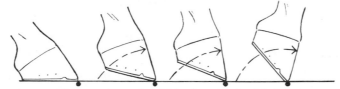

Fig. 71 The arc through which the toe of a hind foot rotates.

Pressure of the foot of an angulated limb behind the body comes too late to produce the optimum drive. Then again a rather straight limb, with a not overangulated hock and stifle, swings more naturally in pendulum fashion from the hip; and although it may not contribute to as long a stride as a more angulated limb, it helps produce more strides per minute. The balance for speed lies in favour of the straighter limb — this applies particularly to sprinters, not only among horses but also in greyhounds. The smaller straight-limbed type can often run away from the bigger, highly angulated one, although the latter do better over longer distances when initial speed is not so important.

A well-developed brachiocephalic muscle is essential, as this is one of the main muscles pulling the front leg forwards. Because it is attached at one end to the skull and neck vertebrae, and at the other to the humerus (Chart 3), it causes the head to move at each alternate contraction and relaxation. This action is most noticeable at the trot when the forelimbs are moving in opposite directions. However, as the forelimb on the other side of the horse is in action and moving in the opposite direction, both the rhomboideus and the cervical part of the serratus ventralis muscles are pulling the neck in the opposite direction. These muscles counterbalance the swinging effect of the brachiocephalic, though, as the horse tires, the head is swung from side to side more markedly.

The Gallop

The gaits so far examined, the walk, trot and pace, are all basically symmetrical, with an even spacing of the intervals between footfalls, and an even distribution of the moments of instability. However, the distinctive feature of the gallop is its lack of symmetry, with a single phase when all four feet are off the ground, and a partial synchronisation of the two fore and two hind limbs (Fig. 72). During the gallop the horse executes a series of springs through the air, mainly as the outcome of rapid contractions of the hind limb retractor muscles, and the extensors of the individual limb joints. The hind feet are driven violently against the ground during the later phase of the stride, but the forefeet will often follow a similar pattern. The horse never has more than two feet on the ground at any one moment and usually only one.

The normal order in which the feet are moved during the gallop is:

RH   LH   RF   LF

alternatively the sequence may be:

LH   RH   LF   RF

At all speeds the period of suspension occurs after the second fore-limb footfall. The body is now projected off the ground by a powerful upthrust of the front foot. This push-up is necessary for the recovery of equilibrium particularly in view of the weight and the rigid spine. In the greyhound, as already explained, the hind limbs can be brought right under the body without the strong upthrust of the forelimbs (Fig. 1), but the propulsion of the horse would not be maintained without the involvement of the leading forelimb.

The closer together the hind feet contact the ground the more efficiently they act as a propulsive unit, but the shorter their period of support of the body (the period when they are both on the ground together is termed the overlap). To counteract this, the stride between the two front feet is close to the maximum possible in order to prolong their support phase for the greatest linear distance.

A galloping horse may project a hind foot as far forwards as its umbilicus, and a forefoot as far as a line dropped perpendicularly

Fig. 72 The gallop: a four-beat gait.

from the muzzle. The foot, however, does not contact the ground until retraction is well under way, i.e. until the limb axis is nearly vertical. The actual impulse provided does not take effect until the body has passed over the vertical limb and the toe is brought into play. The limb is then lifted soon after the vertical has been passed. The complete range of protraction and retraction relative to the hip or shoulder is much greater than in the walk, but the actual ground contact is much shorter.

The foot is necessary for support and to hold the ground while the body passes over it through its own momentum, but it plays little part in facilitating speed through the air, until the body has passed over the limb's centre. It is at this moment that the driving power of the limb can begin to be utilised. The horse propels its body by contraction of the flexor muscles and tendons, driving the toes in and pushing against the ground. The forefoot usually lands on the heel, the weight

Fig. 73 The canter showing a change of lead.

then passing to the wall, the quarters and finally the toe. This is forced
− by the weight of the body − to push against the ground, thus further
aiding forward propulsion. A hind foot, on the other hand, is more
inclined to thrash backwards; in galloping the toe seldom presses
down until the limb has reached the perpendicular. In fast galloping
little other than the toe of the hindfoot makes ground contact. Moderately
firm going increases the efficiency of performance; and the peculiarities
of an animal's gait, dependent partly on conformation, may decide
whether it is a horse that likes heavy going or one that gallops best
on top of the ground.

The canter is more or less a slow gallop. In the gallop there is an
alternation between both front feet and both hind feet, whereas in the
canter the lateral support phase is still in evidence, and the first front
footfall tends to coincide with the last hind footfall (Figs. 73 and 74).

At the walk, trot and pace, the two hind limbs are always moving in
opposite directions, the croup swings from side to side slightly on the
sacroiliac joints, but up and down lumbosacral flexion is practically
non-existent. The side to side swing of the croup adds slightly to the
length of the stride, for at each step by the hind feet the hip is swung
to that side. In the gallop the spine can be flexed slightly in the vertical
plane to bring the hind legs forward at the beginning of the stride. This
occurs as the croup is flexed around the lumbosacral articulation by the
contraction of the hip flexors (psoas major and iliacus). This contraction is accompanied by the reciprocal relaxation of the longissimus
dorsi and middle gluteal (running from the sacrum and ilium to the
major trochanter of the femur). When the foot contacts the ground
the lumbosacral curve flattens by the action of the body weight and
contraction of the longissimus dorsi and middle gluteal muscles. The
psoas major and iliacus give way, absorbing energy and storing it as
potential energy of displacement. As the back straightens the lower
end of the femur is pulled backwards by the passive lifting of the back
of the pelvis; this occurs to complement the contraction of the biceps
femoris muscle.

It is to be emphasised that lumbosacral flexion is of very limited
importance, and the muscles mentioned in the region are mainly concerned with co-operative antagonism above and below the spine in
order to prevent it from bending horizontally or vertically. The spine is
in fact so rigid that any force which would cause it to bend more than a

little might easily result in fracture. This can happen from a tumble or some unusual struggling. It was not an infrequent occurrence when casting horses for operation, though modern anaesthetics and surgical facilities have greatly reduced the risk. Most spinal fractures happen in the thoracic region. The limited spinal movement that does occur in this region takes place between individual thoracic vertebrae, the last thoracic and first lumbar vertebrae, the first three lumbar vertebrae, and between the last lumbar vertebra and the sacrum.

The length of stride at the gallop has been estimated accurately in modern times, and is used in showjumping in the setting and spacing of jumps. A racehorse at full gallop can cover about 7–8 m (6.4–7.3 yds) with each impulse of the hind limbs, and to complete up to a maximum of three strides per second. However, since considerable momentum has been attained by then, the amount of muscular effort is less than if the body were dead weight.

During the gallop the head and neck undergo some oscillation. The downswing requires very little muscular action, the ligamentum nuchae being so arranged that its pull practically equalises the weight of the head and neck when held in the resting position. From here only a slight amount of energy is required to either raise or lower it. Therefore at the gallop when the forelimb hits the ground the head and neck swing down around the articulation of the last cervical and first thoracic

Fig. 74 The canter: a three-beat gait.

vertebra, through a passive swing brought about by normal gravitational force. This movement alters the relationships between certain muscles and the scapula. The rhomboideus and the cervical part of the serratus ventralis now have a more acute angle of insertion onto the scapula. The smaller this angle, and thus the angle of power of muscle on bone, the greater the stabilising effect on that bone. Therefore as the leg contacts the ground the scapula moves down and back as it accepts body weight, and the head swings down. Both actions increase the stabilising effect of the two muscles during the part of the stride when the main function of the limb is support rather than propulsion. At the end of the stride the springing of the forelimb lifts the centre of gravity and the head and neck swing upwards by the elastic rebound of the ligamentum nuchae.

It is appropriate to mention here that the horse takes a breath (inspiration) each time all its legs are off the ground — suspension phase of the stride. It can therefore reach a peak of 180 breaths per minute at a rate of three strides per second. It is while the horse is inspiring air, i.e. during suspension, that the noise commonly associated with roaring is heard. This is very important in diagnosis.

When the feet are on the ground — stance phase — expiration of air occurs.

Limit to Speed

When a horse is moving along at a steady speed the main job that the limbs are performing is the same as when it is at a standstill, namely to support the body against the pull of gravity. The forward propulsive thrust is quite small and the actual speed of movement depends on the frequency of operation of the limbs. As previously mentioned, it is necessary for increasing speed that the hind limbs shall travel backwards faster than the forward speed of the body at that moment. Therefore the retractor muscles must develop more power, implying that these muscles are working below maximum when the horse is moving slowly. Similarly it will be necessary for the forelimbs to move forward sufficiently fast to synchronise with the greater rapidity of movement established by the hind limbs. Therefore as the speed rises the duration of both retraction and protraction decreases, but retraction decreases more so. The rate of stride is increasing and the speed of muscle contraction is increasing, but the speed at which a muscle can contract is limited, and thus the velocity of the action it mediates is also limited. Simply enlarging the muscles, or doubling up their number, will increase the power available but will not increase the speed of action. Speed is increased by altering the relative lengths of the lever arms being operated by the muscles, and by decreasing the length of the power lever arm. Thus throughout evolution there has been a trend towards increased length of limb and shortening of limb muscles so that they attach close to the hip or shoulder joints (the pivots of motion), to increase the swinging speed of the leg and foot. These short muscles, such as the middle gluteal and part of the adductor mass in the hind limb, retract rapidly but with relatively little power. Similarly, protraction is brought about by short muscles such as the psoas major, iliacus and superficial gluteal in the hind limb, again having little power but high speed. The horse however, retains sufficient long axis/high power muscles, such as the triceps femoris and semitendinosus, for bringing about acceleration from a standstill and for moving at slower speeds.

The speed of the leg can also be increased if, at the same time, different muscles extend limb joints in the same direction. The overall propulsive effort, represented by movement of the foot, will exceed the motion produced by any one muscle working alone. The individual effect of each limb section combines to produce an overall higher body speed. We have, therefore, the limb being used as a propulsive lever on the one hand, rotating by extrinsic musculature from the hip or shoulder, and, on the other hand, being used as an extensible strut by intrinsic muscle action extending each individual joint. Maximum speed is reached when both sets of muscles, extrinsic and intrinsic, are exerting their maximum power output, and thus the duration of both protractor and retractor phases of movement is at a minimum.

Speed can only be maintained for as long as the momentum of the body can be kept slightly on the increase, because growing muscle fatigue is liable to tire the limbs until they are no longer able to move faster than the body. The tendency is then for momentum to fall to the extent that the limbs are no longer able to re-establish it. The horse which comes up to win in the last few strides is one which has reserved enough of its energy to make its limbs move faster than the speed of the body at the moment of making the effort.

Coming to a Halt

A limb whose axis is extended in front of the vertical can exert a backward horizontal force which acts as a brake on the body. The time at which it imparts forward momentum is when it has passed the vertical and relinquished its weight carrying role. During a complete stride it can act alternatively as brake and means of propulsion, with a period overlapping both when weight is supported.

Braking depends upon the use of the heels of the fore and hind feet with dorsiflexion of the foot enabling the toes to be raised. In the hind limbs also, hock and stifle flex gently and throw more weight onto the hind feet which are kept as near as possible beneath the belly rather than striding out behind. During the trot or gallop a horse cannot pull up immediately as it can during the slow walk, so it will have to reverse the gait and finally pull up from the walk. Therefore, after a race, it takes time to stop a horse, as it has to reduce speed slowly, through trot and walk, before finally coming to a standstill.

Jumping

Although the downward thrust of the hind feet against the ground is an important factor in galloping it is even more so in jumping (Fig. 75). During galloping the impact of the hind toe with the ground does not require force so much as speed, as the greatest part of the propulsion takes place during the last third of the backward thrust. Whether the animal accelerates or slows down depends upon whether the speed of limb movement is greater or less than the momentum of the body at the time. In addition, each impact of the hind foot with the ground produces a braking effect, since when it lands there is a slow-down while the body travels over the foot. This is accomplished at the cost of momentum, before the foot can begin to make use of the power lying behind it.

When jumping, the amount of power required from the hind limbs depends largely on the speed at which the jump is approached, the momentum of the body, and whether the position of the feet at take-off permits the hind limbs to make their full effort. A clever horse, a clever rider, and someone equally clever at laying out and placing jumps, may make it possible for the horse to arrive at a jump without needing to alter stride, or actually risk charging into the obstacle.

Preparation for the jump begins when the body is supported by the leading foreleg. The front of the animal must now be lifted and the centre of gravity moved back. The experienced jumper uses its head and neck to alter its centre of gravity in order that the weight may concentrate behind its normal position. The front end is pushed into the air by the straightening of the forelimb. The shoulder and elbow extend through the action of the short heads of the triceps on the elbow joint, and the biceps brachii and supraspinatus muscles on the shoulder. Especially important is fetlock extension, through the superficial flexor, but mainly through the more muscular deep flexor. The serratus ventralis contracts to shift the centre of gravity backwards but also to lift the body in relation to the scapula, which is itself rising because of the shoulder extension. The anterior deep pectoral functions here together with the serratus muscle. The epaxial musculature of the back between the croup and neck also contracts strongly, arching the back as much as is possible, and helping to raise the front off the ground.

At the same time as the forehand is being raised the hind limbs are being brought together beneath the body to support the weight. There is practically no period of suspension between the lifting of the forelimb

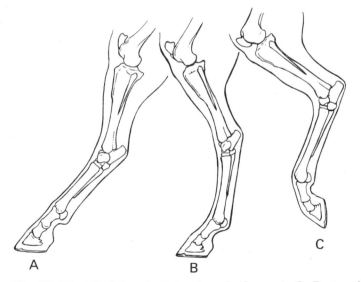

Fig. 75 Hind limb in: A. Extension, B. Support, C. Protraction, at point of take-off for jumping.

and the placing of the first hind foot. The take-off occurs close to the footprint left by the leading forelimb. The horse straightens the hind limbs by extension of stifles and hocks and also fetlocks and hips. The hip is extended by the action of the biceps femoris, semitendinosus and semimembranosus muscles aided by the middle gluteals inserting onto the major trochanter, and the posterior parts of both adductor and gracilis muscles which pass onto the shaft of the femur. The last three of these, because of their short lever arms, are not powerful muscles but muscles of speed. The former group, comprising the bulk of the quarters, are inserted lower down the leg and have a longer lever arm, being more powerful but imparting less speed. We therefore have a situation whereby the movement is started by the long lever-arm muscles, which also provide the strength of pull, but the rapidity of the movement occurs after limb straightening has been started and inertia lessened, this is brought about by the short lever-arm muscles.

The muscles of the quarters also directly extend the stifle and hock joints through the patellar insertion and the tarsal tendon onto the tuber calcis. Stifle joint extension is increased dramatically by contraction of the three vastus muscles of the quadriceps femoris group which extend from the front of the femur, with the rectus femoris also crossing the hip joint so that during contraction it regulates smooth extension of the joint. Hock joint extension is supplemented greatly by the gastrocnemius, and the reciprocal mechanism supplements all the muscles in opening out these two joints. The final impetus to the jump is given by fetlock straightening, mainly through the action of the deep flexor muscle.

The moment the forefoot leaves the ground the forelimbs begin to flex, especially at elbow and knee. These movements are aided by brachiocephalic contraction bringing the limb upwards and forwards. Thus at the moment of take-off the forelimbs will be bent up and the hind limbs fully extended. The force employed has to lift the belly clear of the jump. With double and triple bar jumps the lift has to be greater to carry the body higher before gravity causes it to descend.

When the horse makes its effort, it drives the feet against the ground in order to suddenly straighten its hips, stifles, hocks and fetlocks. The upper parts of the limbs — the quarters, thighs and second thighs — will travel faster than those from the hocks down, because the feet will be planted on the ground until they are lifted by the moving body.

This effect of lifting may even exert a retarding influence, which is best understood when we remember that a man jumps better in light shoes than in heavy boots.

The practised jumper will flex the hocks and stifles in order to bring the feet safely over, or it may kick out behind in order to extend these joints behind the body, mainly through the gastrocnemius muscle and the action of the reciprocal mechanism.

At the same time as the hocks are flexing the forelimbs are extending preparatory to contact with the ground. This contact is made with one extended foreleg followed closely by its fellow placed out in front of the first to give a good base of support. The landing of the second forefoot allows the first to be moved out of the way quickly since it is in the place where the hind feet will come to earth. The hind limbs come down one after the other, but before the second has touched the ground the second forelimb has already pushed off.

The strain upon the joints when a horse lands first on one foot then on the other, as it should do, is very heavy because practically the whole weight plus the influence of gravity falls on one foot. Frequently the fetlock comes to the ground, and if the horse lands on its heel and the toe turns upwards, the strain exerted on the navicular bone by the deep flexor tendon may easily fracture it or cause damage to the tendon. When landing in this position, the forefoot having reached too far ahead, or if it has skidded on slippery turf, there is no hope of the body using the limb as a spoke and passing over it. It is left to the other forefoot to make a rapid advance. In many instances when a forefoot skids like this, particularly during a hurdle race, the body sinks in front and the second forelimb is unable to straighten out. Instead it doubles up at the knee and the horse falls.

Horses were not originally designed as jumpers, as is evident from the fixed state of the spine. The fore-end is heavy, as are the head and neck. In order to be a good jumper, a horse ideally needs long, but not heavy, limbs, a body which is slim, light and streamlined, and should be lightly built in front and strong at the rear. Although it will not profit as a jumper by carrying heavy shoulders, too heavy a head or too wide a front, it certainly helps if it has a well laid-back shoulder with sound forelimbs and feet. However, watching the winners of competitions today, it is clear successful athletes appear in all shapes and sizes.

9 Concussion and its Effect on Movement

Being a major factor in lameness, concussion (axial compression force) is worthy of more serious consideration here. As an essential element of every stride and movement, especially at speeds faster than the walk, it is accentuated by camber, surface and hardness of the ground beneath the foot. It is the force sent vertically up the leg every time a limb strikes the ground. Thus the limbs of a horse jumping down from a field onto a hard road will evidently absorb concussion to a degree that could easily end in injury, but the concussion absorbed by a fit, shod horse while trotting fast along a hard road may not be that much less.

Concussion is not only affected by condition of the ground surface, but also by fitness because exercise tends to strengthen and harden the body from the flaccid unfit state of the sedentary animal. An uneven, stony or pot-holed road may force the joints to take strain to one side or the other, bending them in a way that could cause injury. A steep camber may have the same effect.

It is surprising how many marginally lame horses show increased signs on uneven surfaces, not just on stones that may contact the sole, but simply from trotting up- or downhill. All these factors have their own importance when trying to diagnose lameness. Horses with splints and sore shins are often more lame trotting downhill on a firm surface, while those with muscular problems may be far worse when climbing a soft bank. Similarly, muscular injuries can have serious implications for swimming horses. Failure to appreciate this sometimes leads to accidents. For example, horses with back muscle injuries may be unable to swim, leaving them susceptible to drowning.

The important thing when meeting concussion is that the horse's anatomy be given the optimum chance of dealing with it as nature intended, i.e. without injury. This is one of the reasons why horses are shod; it is the purpose of the shoe to protect the foot from undue wear, to limit concussion and to spread its effect through the structures of the foot in a natural way. To achieve this the foot must be properly levelled, the frog, digital cushion, cartilages and blood plexuses must all function normally, and there must be no pressure on sensitive tissues or bruising from nail or shoe on structures which may become inflamed or infected.

In relation to concussion, the critical aspect of the well-fitted shoe is the level of the bearing surface and the way the foot strikes the ground. The level of the foot must be correct, otherwise a level shoe will not meet the ground on a level plane. For this reason it is necessary that a horse be walked and trotted for the farrier before shoeing, so that he

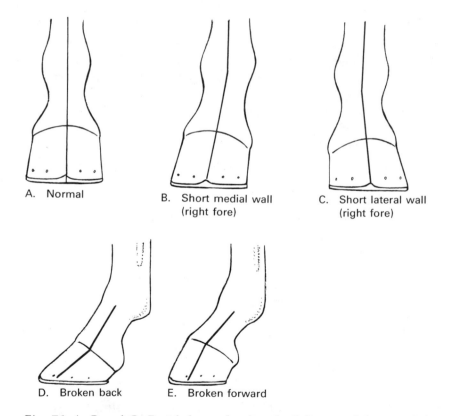

Fig. 76 A, B and C. Foot balance showing the influence of short medial and lateral walls. D and E. Broken foot axis.

can see the shape and action and trim the foot accordingly, ensuring it is level when shod. It is also imperative that the finished shoe itself be level, otherwise the whole balance of the leg is disturbed. Certain types of shoe contain areas for providing grip on slippery surfaces, it is not uncommon for these to wear unevenly, thus leaving a shoe which is unstable, and possibly resulting in injury to joints directly affected.

Follow the plane of the bearing surface in Figs. 76A, B and C, and note how a shortening of the wall either medially or laterally upsets the whole balance of the limb in relation to the ground and influences the path of concussive forces travelling upwards. It also may affect the way forces coming down the limb − from the weight of the body − are received. Lameness commonly ensues in these cases and is almost inevitable if the fault is not corrected. Also note how elongation of the toe, lowering of the heel and dumping of the front of the foot all affect the foot/pastern axis and, similarly, cause lameness.

In certain cases, foot balance may be disturbed because of inherent faulty conformation of the animal. Deviations at the fetlock or knee may cause the bearing angle of foot and ground to be unlevel. The consequent effect may mean that concussion is absorbed mainly by the structures below the faulty joint, thereby causing serious limitations to the animal's ability to perform. As with the human athlete, it is vital that this imbalance be altered by corrective shoeing when possible, even if this means the animal spending its life wearing shoes with outer and inner bars of a different thickness. The important thing is that the animal be protected from the effects of its own, perhaps slight, anatomical problem so that it can lead a useful, and, as far as possible, a natural life.

Concussion is met by the limb and body in the following sequence:

a. The foot − in particular the frog, digital cushion, cartilages etc. allow for a certain amount of absorbtion and are designed to limit the effect on each structure involved.
b. The backward inclination of the pastern and its tendoligamentous supports assist this.
c. The construction of the fetlock and sesamoids with the strong ligamentous bonding and tendinous support helps save these structures and steer concussive forces up through the cannon.

    d. The knee and hock act as shock absorbers.

    e. The angulation of the elbow/shoulder joints in front and the hock/stifle/hip joints behind play their part as already explained.

    f. The muscle masses of the upper limb absorb concussion.

    g. Finally the body and spine are affected.

It is evident that any weakness on this anatomical line can lead to injury in the region where it exists. Thus, if the frontal angulation of the limb when it meets the ground is away from the perpendicular, the site where weakness exposes itself is usually where a perpendicular line from the centre point of ground contact emerges through either aspect of the limb. The result may be sprain, strain or fracture of any of the structures involved − it is the most common cause of splints in mature animals.

Even when conformation is ideal, however, there is never any way of fully preventing the possiblity that a horse will put its foot in a hole when travelling at speed. Tendon injuries, too, may occur as a result of a limb being overstretched mechanically − on landing awkwardly after a jump, for example. But these injuries are also the legacy of faulty training techniques, of too much hurry in getting animals fit, and they may result as secondary conditions when other mechanical limitations on movement, such as muscle damage, puts an undue strain on the tendons.

10 The Muscular System and Movement

Three main types of fibre have been identified in equine skeletal muscle (distinct from cardiac muscle, found only in the heart, and smooth muscle, which is located in organs such as the bowel) designated as Type 1, Type 2a and Type 2b (Fig. 77). It is suggested that athletic ability is related to the distribution of different fibre types in the animal's muscle. Type 1 fibres are slow-twitch, red fibres which have a slow speed of contraction. They exhibit little fatigue and animals with a predominance of Type 1 fibres are likely to be best in endurance events.

Type 2a fibres are fast-twitch white fibres which fatigue readily. These are used for short powerful bursts of activity and are called low oxidative muscle because of a lower capacity for using oxygen. Type 2b fibres are high oxidative, resist fatigue better and are used for more sustained activity. All three types exist within the same muscle body and the relative proportions of each decide the performance type; sprinter, stayer, etc.

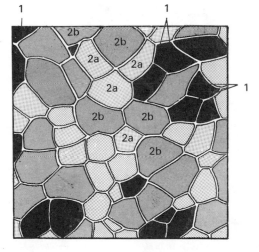

Fig. 77 Equine skeletal muscle showing the three main types of muscle fibre: Type 1 (slow-twitch red fibres). Type 2a (fast-twitch white fibres [low oxidative]). Type 2b (fast-twitch white fibres [high oxidative]).

Concussion is directly influenced by primary muscle injury, which is often ignored because the lameness the injury causes soon passes off. The reason is that the injured area is taken out of use by the body, and action of the affected limb is altered to accommodate it. Thus it is commonly found that an injury to the long head of the triceps brachii results in the leg being used in a way that avoids or reduces the effective working of this muscle. The result is a detectable change in limb action, with the straight extension/flexion process being generally altered to a movement that may exhibit some abduction or rotation. If only a small segment of muscle has ruptured, then the dynamic effect of the injury may be minimal. In any case, the effect is to shorten the potential stretch of the muscle, or muscle fibres, involved. The affected muscle is therefore held as if partially contracted and the influence on limb dynamics is to place a greater strain on the less elastic tendons (in the case of the forelimb); it may also cause deviation in protraction in a manner that interferes with proper placement of the foot on the ground. It is necessary to stress, however, that the extent of any muscular injury may be so slight that the changes which are described above are barely perceptible. Their influence nevertheless can be highly significant.

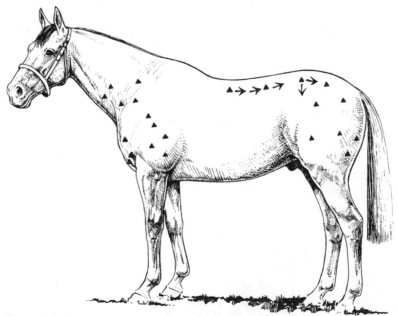

Fig. 78 The most common sites of muscular injury.

It is recognised that the size and strength of muscle fibres increase with training, therefore the greatest incidence of muscular injury occurs when these are less than fully strengthened. Muscular injuries are divided into two types: primary injury, by far the most common, due to uncomplicated muscle fibre rupture as previously mentioned, and secondary muscle damage, which is usually associated with underlying bony disturbance. The latter is an important consideration because it is not uncommon to find underlying fractures associated with gross muscular damage in areas such as the pelvis. However, it should also be remembered that when such fractures have repaired − as they quite commonly do in the pelvis − the animal may not become fully sound until the muscular damage has been corrected. It is far from certain, contrary to common belief, that muscular injuries will correct themselves without treatment. In fact, the reverse is more generally true, and where cartilage and bone formation is found in muscle it is most probably always preceded by simple primary injuries which were not effectively treated.

Atrophy (wasting) is a feature of chronic muscular injury, and is particularly seen in the shoulder and upper pelvic areas as flat or shrunken muscle. It is due to a decrease in volume of an unused muscle, occurring after it has been injured or sometimes when its nerve supply has been directly interfered with. Atrophy will occur more generally when an area is immobilised, as after the application of a cast, etc., and it is also sometimes seen as an expression of malnutrition and senility.

Imbalance of muscular co-ordination can also cause injury, even fracture, when the pull of opposing muscle groups occurs out of synchronisation. This can arise from sudden unbalanced movement, as when a horse plunges or tries to save itself when it slips up; or, as already said, when an animal is recumbent under anaesthesia. Injury may occur, too, when a limb suddenly has to be projected fowards in order to prevent a fall.

The conditions known as nutritional or exertional myopathies are not mechanical muscular injuries and do not really apply here. However, their existence has a significant part to play in muscular injury diagnosis that is made most efficiently with experienced use of a Faradic-type machine. These machines are diagnostic, and also an essential part of successful therapy. In fact, it is probably true to say that few primary muscle injuries are fully cured without Faradic-type treatment.

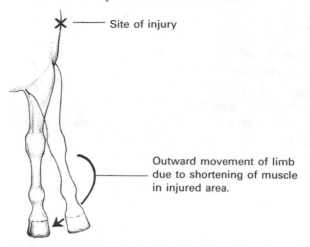

X ——— Site of injury

Outward movement of limb
due to shortening of muscle
in injured area.

Fig. 79 Altered forelimb flight due to injury in the long head of the triceps muscle behind the shoulder.

The normal action of any horse is therefore influenced by muscular damage acquired during the training period. Formerly the exercise of strapping, a routine part of stable management, had the effect of keeping muscle supple and helped disperse the normal waste products of contraction which build up after physical exercise. Now that this is no longer routine, trainers accept changes in a horse's action as part of the normal training pattern and are not concerned unless the animal displays overt lameness. The consequence is that many horses are eventually rendered unsound and subsequently disappear from training altogether. Prevention could well eliminate a great deal of this.

The modern way to monitor muscle health in trained horses is with Faradic-type current. The method, though diagnostic as well as curative, is, surprisingly, not a routine element of racehorse management. Muscle needs to be monitored on a regular basis; if it were, primary muscle lameness would be reduced in incidence and a great deal of secondary lameness might also be prevented.

It should be understood that a whole range of equipment is now marketed for the treatment of muscular injuries. It is important to know that many of these only relieve pain and stimulate circulation of the part. Their effect is palliative and short term. The injury is unlikely to be cured fully without the mechanical encouragement of electrical stimulation, which ensures that the treated tissues return to effective use.

11   Conformation and Soundness

The purpose of this chapter is to link conformation with the common weaknesses in equine anatomy, and to join this view with standard concepts of conformation.

It must be emphasised at the outset that many horses whose basic shape is far from ideal win races and other competitions. However, no sensible person buys an animal with an obvious fault except with full knowledge and in expectation that it will fulfil its use despite the fault.

It is arguable that the basic construction of the limbs — with a single digit taking a great deal of concussion — is less than desirable. However, there is no way this basic fact can be changed to order. And it might also be considered that the great majority of injuries may derive from factors which are within our capacity to eliminate. With regard to this, the reference is not to hard or uneven ground, but to methods and care of training, shoeing, stabling and animal management.

General Conformation

To begin with, it is important that the individual anatomic characteristics fit the required use of the animal. Thus a working draught horse will have greater substance and more powerful muscle development in the areas likely to be used in its work. The shoulder will be relatively upright and strongly developed, the neck short and heavily muscled with plenty of support for the collar. In the athletic horse, on the other hand, the balance of the relative parts of the body to each other — head and neck, thorax and forelimbs, abdomen and hind limbs — is vital, and different. If there is too much weight in the head and neck it displaces the centre of gravity forward and makes the front end of the body less stable. If the back is too long it moves the centre of gravity backwards and also increases the risk of spinal injury.

Short limbs with the shoulder and quarter highly muscled are desireable in a draught horse, but a sprinter may also have relatively short limbs and will require a different type of muscle fibre in its well-developed shoulder and quarter. So all judgment is relative and must, as stated, depend on the animal's required use as well as being based on its conformational peculiarities.

The Head

First examine the animal at rest, standing well back and inspecting each side and viewpoint individually. Then come closer and, starting at the head, note the alignment of the incisor teeth. In a parrot mouth, the upper row overshoots the lower and this is an hereditary unsoundness; it is conformation which should render a stallion unfit for stud duties — though this is not always the case. Such conformation may have an effect on the animals ability to graze, and would thus have an influence on its life span, though it is surprising how well many horses do with very badly made mouths. The condition occurs in varying degrees from correct alignment to complete over- or under-shooting of the incisor teeth.

A great deal has been written and said about conformation of the head, and different breeds and types have recognised characteristics which are preferred for showing purposes. However, from a practical point of view, the set of the eyes, the size of the ears, the breadth of the forehead are all variable and relative, as long as there is no evident

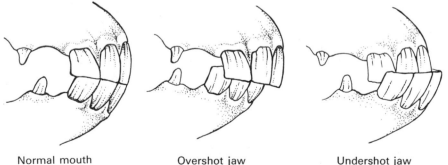

Normal mouth   Overshot jaw   Undershot jaw
                      (parrot mouth)

Fig. 80 Jaw alignment.

abnormality seen. A wall-eyed horse is often said to be volatile and quick-tempered, but many such animals are not, and there is no evidence that vision is in any way limited by such an evident blemish. Horses with loppy ears are sometimes thought to be phlegmatic, but some very good racing families are lop-eared and none the less successful for it either.

We are advised that the space between the mandibles should be broad and deep, as there is a suggested correlation between the condition known as laryngeal hemiplegia, or roaring, and anatomical restriction of this area. However, many clinical sufferers have a conformation of this part which is in line with the ideals advocated, besides which clinical theory does not relate the specific pathology to nerve damage in the laryngeal area, but farther afield at the entrance to the chest where the recurrent laryngeal nerve turns around a blood vessel. The important thing to remember is that the condition is known to be hereditary, and it is about time known roarers and whistlers were not permitted to stand at stud. This applies to mares as well as stallions, though, inevitably, a stallion's defects can have a far wider influence on breeding.

The Neck

Every horse must have free use of its neck, which should be strong and balanced, with adequate muscular development to allow good extension of the front limbs. The vertebrae of the neck are particularly prone to minor mechanical misalignments which are not usually detectable on x-ray, though more serious injuries are known to occur. The most common problem is thought to place pressure on emerging nerves, this in turn affects muscular contraction and often leads to faulty front limb protraction. This can originate from the region of the atlas and axis, the joints with the greatest degree of movement in the neck, though any other cervical vertebra may also be involved. As already indicated, problems of this nature occur at all levels of the spine.

In veterinary circles, there has been a great deal of scepticism regarding the occurrence, diagnosis and manipulation of spinal-derived lameness of this nature. However, the simple fact is that the incidence is high, lameness is pronounced — if not to the extent that might be detected by the inexperienced eye — and manipulation is very successful. The difficulty is that the pathological basis is not fully defined, and it is possible that the degree of lameness may well baffle the modern technological approach to diagnosis. It is accepted that the extent of natural movement between vertebrae is minimal, and this fact alone accounts for a certain amount of the scepticism. Yet the influences of the condition are easily detectable on surface manipulation and successful treatment leads to their disappearance in a significant percentage of cases. Jumping horses in particular suffer from it, and trainers will freely admit that certain horses cannot jump (or even race to form on the flat) when they have back problems. In fact many trainers have their horses manipulated routinely before races.

It is imperative that the muscles supporting the spinal column be strong, free of injury and adequately developed in all regions. The influence when any of these are injured is for the pull on the column to become uneven and bony problems develop as a result, evidently pulling solid structures marginally out of alignment with ensuing lameness. Primary muscular injury in the neck is quite common (Fig. 77), as it is also in the lumbar and sacral regions of the back.

The Forelimb

The Foot

Starting from the ground, the foot should be full and well formed with no hint of contraction; its natural bearing with the ground should be level and place no pressure on other remote structures such as fetlocks,

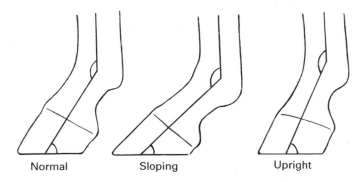

Normal   Sloping   Upright

Fig. 81 Lateral view of foot/pastern axis.

tendons or knees. The bearing axis should neither break forward or backwards when a line is drawn along the front of the foot and continued over the pastern to the fetlock. In the forelimb the ideal foot/pastern angle is 45–50 degrees and in the hind 50–55 degrees (Fig. 81). The toe should not be short and the sole should be concave and removed from contact with the shoe or ground on its bearing surface inside the white line. The heel, which should be neither too high nor too low, should be full and expanded, with no contraction of the frog, which should contact the ground when the foot bears weight.

The Pastern

The pastern should follow the foot axis and break neither back or forward from it. Where it does so, there is undue strain on the structures affected and the only way of correcting this is often at the foot. If the line breaks backwards, the heel may need to be raised or the toe shortened; where it breaks forward, the opposite is the case. Whichever way, when the axis is broken there is pressure on the coffin and pastern joints and a greater chance of high and low ringbone occurring. It also places greater stress on the fetlock support system.

It is also important for the pastern to have length in proportion to the size of the animal. A pastern that is too long is weak and subjects the fetlock and the suspensory apparatus to undue strain. A pastern that is too short may place greater strain on the bony structures of the limb.

The Fetlock

The fetlock should be strong and give the impression of being well bonded. It is critical to the soundness of the animal, for reasons already discussed, that this joint be constructed in such a way as to take the impact of concussion up the limb as well as the forces imposed downwards by the weight of the body above. For this reason all the ligaments and tendons involved in the formation of the joint must be perfectly constructed and properly angled. If the fetlock joint is too upright, there is greater concussion on the bony surfaces of the joint itself, as well as on the cannon and knee; if it is too angulated, the ligaments supporting the joint come under too much pressure when maximum weight is applied to the limb.

The Cannon

The cannon is ideally short in relation to the overall size of the body because a long cannon is less strong structurally than a shorter one of the same diameter. The way the tendons are bound onto the back of the cannon is important, and may give an indication of how strong they are; short strong tendons are less likely to give trouble than long weak ones. There is no doubt that a cannon conformation that is well proportioned and properly balanced will generally indicate strength and soundness.

The Knee

The knee is a critical joint in the forelimb and its construction is vital to the overall strength of the limb. Owing to its upright conformation, the bones of the knee bear a great deal of the concussive forces coming up the leg. It is therefore important that the joint be balanced in a medial-lateral direction, i.e., that it neither deviates in or out when viewed from the front. Also, from a side view, the knee should not bear forward or backward, though forward deviation is less objectionable, being easier on limb structures, and some trainers actually favour this conformation. The danger is that it will cause forward instability when an animal is landing from a jump, though this seldom proves to be the case. On the other hand, backward deviation is a particularly bad conformation, bringing forces to bear on the bones of the knee which they are unlikely to withstand longterm.

Open knees are a sign of immaturity and are most commonly seen in foals, yearlings and two-year-olds. In this condition, enlargement of the epiphyseal plates of the upper end of the large metacarpal and lower end of the radius is marked. Generally, as long as the diet is balanced and the animal prevented from injuring the knee by galloping on hard ground, the condition will resolve itself in time. In a sense the presence of open knees is a warning of immaturity and patience is advised before proceeding with the animal's training.

The Elbow and Shoulder

Injury to the elbow and shoulder joints is less common, partly because of their angulated relationship with the lower limb. As neither joint

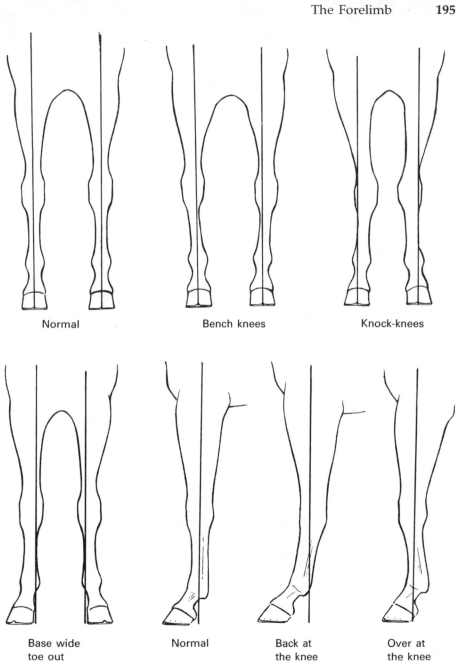

Normal   Bench knees   Knock-knees

Base wide
toe out   Normal   Back at
the knee   Over at
the knee

Fig. 82 Forelimb conformation.

ever comes into a straight line with the rest of the limb, even in full extension, these are subjected to less direct effect from concussion. Occasionally separation of the radius and ulna may occur, or direct injury to the shoulder from striking an obstacle. However the most common problem in this region is primary muscle injury and this does not relate to angulation of the shoulder and scapula. Inevitably, however, overall angulation has a direct effect on concussion and the line of the scapular spine should ideally parallel the foot/pastern axis. Otherwise the preferred angulation depends on whether a short, rapid or powerful stride is required or a long, slower more enduring one. It is the choice of sprinter against stayer, of strength against elegance. The angle of the shoulder can depend on the length of the humerus, which can vary proportionately — though the angle of the shoulder joint itself is fairly stable.

Horses with elbows set far back — due to undue length of the humerus — bear increased concussion of the forelimb, and on the spine, and this is usually transmitted to the rider. Those with a well set-back scapula have a longer stride, are more comfortable to ride, and more elegant to observe.

The Thorax

The thorax should provide adequate space for the heart and lungs and the set of the forelimbs should be neither too close nor too far apart. Narrow animals will often require a breast girth, because of a tendency for the saddle to slip backwards during exercise.

The withers and dorsal spine are important in so much as they represent the most rigid part of the back and any weakness may indicate inability to carry weight or remain sound if asked to jump. The support area for the saddle should ideally be strong and well formed, and shaped in such a way that there is no hard contact between back and saddle, with the rider's weight being distributed evenly off the bony column.

The Back

The length and muscular strength of the back are important. While a roach back may be unsightly it is not necessarily weak, though a dipped back has an evident inherent weakness which is likely to cause problems in the long term. A short back is inevitably stronger while a long one is more subject to trouble.

When mounting, remember that the best method is always from a block or by vaulting. Damage to the back can easily be caused by adding all of a rider's weight to one side of the spine, pulled through stirrup and girth. This is a particular consideration with horses which have already suffered from back problems.

The Hind Limb

The hind limb up as far as the hock is similar in design and construction to the fore, except that the ideal foot/pastern axis is, as said earlier, in the range of 50—55 degrees to the ground.

The Hock

The hock, because of the manner in which it operates, needs to be very well bonded, and this is a quality that is best judged by eye from the side, front and rear of the joint. If the ligamentous bonding appears weak at the lower rear of the joint it is likely to indicate weakness in the curb region. If the joint is too upright it means there will be greater stress on the tuber calcis and the structures attached to it. Pulling or rupture of the Achilles tendon may result, or the superficial flexor tendon may slip off the hock. If the joint is too bent, the structures attached to the hock are also under pressure.

A hock that deviates to the inner or outer side is inevitably placing a stress on all the bony structures of the limb. As the hock itself is significantly involved in concussion absorbtion, its small bones are more prone to injury when they meet it in anything other than a straight line. The result of deviation may be bone or bog spavin, depending on the exact structures which are involved.

The Stifle and Hip

The stifle and hip joints are protected to an extent from the direct effects of concussion both by their angulation with the leg and by the reciprocal apparatus. However, the stifle is subject to the great pulling force of the quarter muscles and is more commonly injured than the

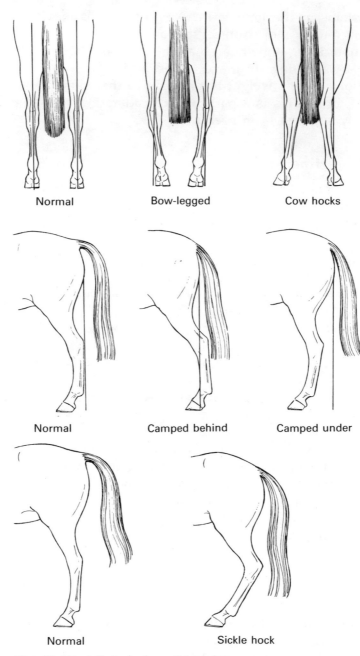

Fig. 83 Hind limb conformation.

shoulder because of its construction. Injury to this joint is expressed by the accumulation of synovial fluid and lameness at the walk. Injury of the hip is less common.

As has already been pointed out, there is a direct relationship between the angulation of the hock and stifle joints, so that an upright hock will also mean an upright stifle. This type of conformation in the stifle is more likely to lead to pathological locking of the joint, especially in immature animals.

The Pelvis

The pelvic roof is an area which is subject to the direct mechanical forces of hind limb action. The result is that muscular injuries are common on the upper part of the quarter and in the large muscle masses running down to the stifle. Displacement of the sacrum is not an uncommon occurrence and the sacro-iliac joint is very often involved in injuries to the area. It is also not unknown for the tail to be broken and any abnormality in its use may indicate more serious disruption of spinal function.

Movement and Action

Finally the animal is judged at the walk and trot and even, in the show ring, at the canter and gallop. It is important to watch the action from all angles, but particularly from front and behind. The stance and uniformity of the body is critical. There must be no favouring of a limb and no unevenness in the bony and muscular structures when viewed from any side. Particular note should be made of atrophy, or wasting, of individual muscles in the neck, shoulder, back, quarter and thigh. The level of the pelvis on both sides is gauged by standing directly behind the horse; as the animal walks away the movement should be level.

At the trot, the movement of the forelimbs should be even and balanced, with no deviation of the limb out or in towards the body, except where this is a natural conformational fault — in which case the judgement will be critical. From the side, the stride length should be even and flowing, the whole movement rhythmic and appealing to the eye. The same applies to the hind limbs; there should be evenness

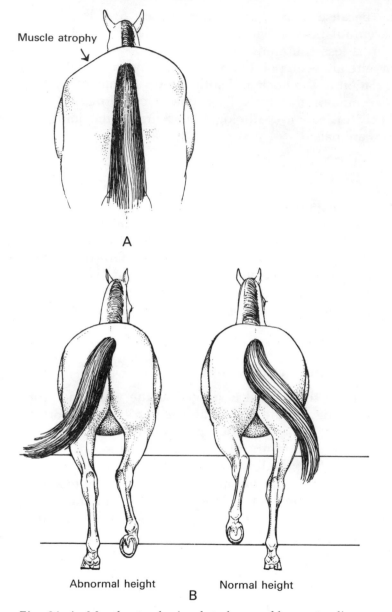

Muscle atrophy

A

Abnormal height   Normal height

B

Fig. 84 A. Muscle atrophy in gluteal area of horse standing square.
B. The flight of the hind legs at trot. The foot and hock should rise
equally both sides, but a lame horse may not lift its hock or foot to a
normal height.

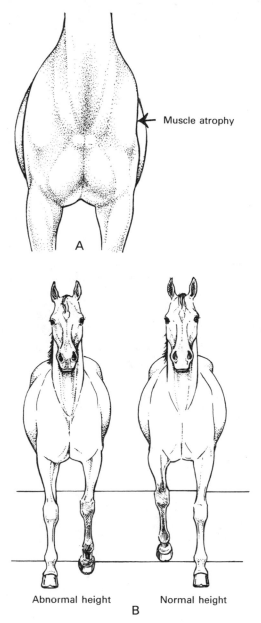

Muscle atrophy

A

Abnormal height   Normal height

B

Fig. 85 A. Muscle atrophy at the shoulder. B. Abnormal stride length may be recognised by failure to extend, or lift, a limb to the normal height.

of the pelvis, and tracking should be equal in both limbs from the side. Flexion and extension must be free and uninhibited — both hocks and feet rising to the same height from the ground — with no break in movement; the leg fully protracted in extension. There should be no undue wear on the toe or heel of the hind or front feet when picked up.

In movement, the length of the stride is fairly uniform between similar-type horses and has little influence on the rate of progression because when the front foot lands slightly farther forward than usual it is also farther from the shoulder than if the stride were shorter. It therefore takes slightly longer for the body to travel over the foot than when the stride is shorter. Accordingly the hind limb has to wait a little and the number of strides per minute is reduced, though each stride may carry the body further.

As far as speed is concerned, it is a matter of whether a smaller number of longer strides cover the ground more quickly than a greater number of shorter ones. Of course, genetics, especially in the human sphere, leads us to believe that a big athlete who can move his or her legs quickly has an advantage over a shorter one with the same speed of limb. So, quick long strides do prove more effective than quick short ones. The difference in the case of the horse is that we consider bigger horses to be undesirable and less able to stay sound. Therefore, by breeding horses to a limited size it is possible to eliminate the influence size may have on speed, in contrast to the human athlete where increasing size and stride length is an important aspect of improving performance.

Index

Page numbers in *italics* refer to illustrations